THE PUZZLER'S PARADISE

THE PUZZLER'S PARADISE

From the Garden of Eden to the Computer Age

Helene Hovanec

With a Foreword by Margaret Farrar

PADDINGTON
PRESS LTD
NEW YORK & LONDON

To Erik

and the six hours at the Library of Congress

Library of Congress Cataloging in Publication Data

Hovanec, Helene, 1941–
  The Puzzler's Paradise.

  Bibliography: p.
  Includes index.
  1.Puzzles – History. I.Title.
GV1493.H64   793.7′3   78-6508
ISBN 0 7092 0321 7
ISBN 0 448 22423 2 (U.S. and Canada only)

Copyright © 1978 Office du Livre
All rights reserved

Filmset, printed and bound in the United States
Cover Illustration by Ken Cox

IN THE UNITED STATES
PADDINGTON PRESS
Distributed by
GROSSET & DUNLAP

IN THE UNITED KINGDOM
PADDINGTON PRESS

IN CANADA
Distributed by
RANDOM HOUSE OF CANADA LTD.

IN SOUTHERN AFRICA
Distributed by
ERNEST STANTON (PUBLISHERS) (PTY.) LTD.

⟩CONTENTS⟨

FOREWORD

by Margaret Farrar

To be reminded that puzzles have a long and illustrious history on this small planet is a refreshing experience. All the way from the riddle of the Sphinx down through the ages, the magnetism of puzzles is evident in man's constant search for answers.

Here is the story, informally and delightfully told, of the earliest known puzzles, their progress from ancient times to the present and how they changed with the times from an art form practiced by the few to recreation for the multitudes.

What is more, here are hundreds of examples of all sorts of puzzles typifying the rich progression of word play that amused and edified former generations: the riddles so widespread among ancient civilizations, enigmas of ancient and respectable origin, palindromes, logogriphs, conundrums, puns, cryptograms, transpositions, Sam Loyd's stumpers, charades, acrostics and many others in endless variety.

Our times are, of course, reflected in the popular double crostic and the all-encompassing crossword which, since 1924, has been a worldwide phenomenon. "A bittersweet mixture of bewilderment and discovery," commented Ivor Brown on the cryptic variety practiced in England.

"Man is a puzzle-solving animal," propounded Ronald Arbuthnott Knox (1888-1957), Roman Catholic priest and translator of the Bible. A man fond of epigrams and paradoxes, an expert in palindromes and word squares, he knew whereof he spoke.

Helene Hovanec also knows the world of puzzles as a dedicated solver and researcher. Her retelling of the story cannot fail to interest and entertain the myriads of people who enjoy words.

7

╳INTRODUCTION╳

IN PRAISE OF PUZZLES

Although it's fashionable to blame mothers for our assorted hang-ups, I can only thank mine for leading me down the path of passionate puzzling, for it was she who bought me the activity books that started me on my way.

I loved the smell of a new book, especially one you were encouraged to write in. There were pictures to color, mazes to fill in, stories to read and, best of all, word puzzles to solve. I devoured the puzzles; I would finish a book in a few hours and wail loudly for more. I must have owned every puzzle book published during my childhood years. I never tired of them.

I muddled through pubescence and early adolescence as awkward as my peers—too old for children's puzzles, but too young for crosswords in the newspapers. That period is blurred in my memory; I somehow survived without puzzles and I'm still trying to repress it. Then, in my sixteenth year a series of events occurred that sped me on the path toward total addiction!

First, I discovered *The New York Times* crossword puzzle. My social studies teacher required all students to purchase *The Times*, read it from cover to cover, and remember enough of the contents to pass a daily current events quiz. Thoroughly exhausted by digesting "all the news that was fit to print," I one day decided to amuse myself with the crossword. Nothing in my prior experience had prepared me for the frustration I was about to feel. I had never seen such clues before: Egyptian sun god, printer's measure, extinct bird, waste allowance, three-toed sloth. On good days I was able to fill in a maximum of three words.

I might have been sufficiently discouraged at this point to give up puzzles forever had it not been for a second fortuitous event. A brilliant puzzlist decided to become my mentor. I was working part-time at an advertising agency in New York City. The art director there was not only a creative genius, but he did *The Times* puzzle every day—in ink! The admiration I displayed for his amazing skill so flattered him that he single-handedly undertook to educate me in puzzle solving. He gave me hints on attacking the puzzle, made up word lists for me of repeated clues and taught me to understand the definitions. In no time at all I flourished under his tutelage until I could complete the puzzle independently. My confidence zoomed. I was a pro, ace, tops, a-one!

Success with *The Times* puzzle crystallized my feelings about the joy of puzzle solving. I decided to become a total puzzle person and I'm happy to report that I've succeeded in my goal. I subscribe to specialized puzzle magazines and purchase several mass-market publications solely for their puzzle columns. I joined the National Puzzlers' League and was one of the prime movers responsible for reinstituting puzzle conventions. I construct puzzles for magazines, schools and library programs. Like the proverbial drinker who could find a bar on the moon, I manage to find puzzles in the most unexpected places—art galleries, gift boutiques and clothing stores. Puzzles are one of my favorite pastimes and I intend never to break the habit!

I used to believe that my passion for puzzles was rather extreme. However, the proliferation of puzzle activities in the past few years convinced me that puzzling is one of our most popular pastimes. New puzzle magazines have sprung up, crossword competitions are well attended, Scrabble tournaments are spotlighted in news programs and the crossword grid has become a chic motif, featured on clothing, tote bags and even shower curtains.

Interestingly, this renaissance of puzzles has not focused on the heritage behind them. Many puzzlers are unaware of the puzzles of the past or of the puzzle greats who left their individual stamp on puzzle evolution or of how puzzles have permeated into other leisure-time areas.

I felt that a book highlighting puzzles through the ages would be welcomed by all who wanted to know more about puzzles but didn't know who to ask. *The Puzzler's Paradise* is by no means a complete documentation of everything that has occurred in puzzles since the beginning of time. Rather, it is an attempt to create a composite picture of the influence of puzzles throughout the ages. For all the people who are passionate puzzlers this book is written in praise of puzzles.

PUZZLE ORIGINS

Tracing the historical roots of puzzles is as revealing as constructing one's family tree. In investigating family lineage the blood relationships between generations yesterday and today are not always readily apparent; sometimes in-depth examination is necessary before the particular elements connecting a family's heritage can be recognized. Yet the ties that bind definitely do exist.

So it is with puzzles. Most of today's puzzles differ dramatically from their predecessors; yet like families, the branches joining the past and present are visible, albeit faint. The roots are there and exploring them can help us to appreciate the unique heritage of today's puzzles and the refinements which have occurred over the centuries.

Riddles

All puzzles, from riddles and anagrams to crosswords and word searches, embody the twin elements of disguise and discovery. Throughout history, puzzle constructors have striven to produce puzzles that simultaneously conceal the answers yet cry out to be solved, while solvers have risen to the challenge of pitting their own ingenuity against that of the constructors. The underlying assumption is that both constructor and solver will derive pleasure from their pastime.

With Oedipus, who well deserves the title of "the first great puzzle solver," the question of how much pleasure he derived from his puzzle activities is almost as complex as the complex which Freud named after him! Oedipus was the hero who prevented the ruination of Thebes by answering the seemingly unsolvable riddle propounded by the Sphinx: "What walks on four legs in the morning, two legs in the afternoon and three legs in the evening?" Prior to Oedipus's appearance in Thebes, scores of would-be solvers had been stumped by the riddle and put to death by the Sphinx for their failure to solve it. Oedipus, however, was not to be daunted. "It is man who crawls as a child, walks upright in his prime and uses a cane in old age," he answered boldly. The Sphinx's power over the city was instanta-

Oedipus and the Sphinx, a puzzling perception by Gustave Moreau. Oedipus's ability to answer the difficult riddle of the Sphinx earned him the reputation as the "first puzzle solver." Although the correct solution had tragic consequences for both solver and constructor, the art of puzzling continued to flourish.

neously thwarted and the Thebans rejoiced in their new savior. Not to be outdone, the Sphinx committed suicide by throwing herself from her rock. As his reward, Oedipus went on to marry the queen of Thebes, who, of course, turned out to be his mother (he had already unwittingly killed the king, his father), and events go downhill from there. Fortunately, puzzle makers and solvers haven't always met with such dire fates, but a few of the ancients seem to have had a rougher time of it than most, as they took their riddling rather more seriously than we do.

Riddles would have to be considered the oldest form of puzzles. They are to be found throughout the mythologies of many cultures and were important in ancient religion and philosophy as one of the vehicles through which the sages expressed their wisdom. Primitive peoples were obsessed with imagery and looked upon the ability to pose and solve riddles as an indication of great mental agility.

The Philistines' answer to Samson's unique riddle and the warrior's scathing reply, as pictured in rebus form in a children's hieroglyphic Bible from the early nineteenth century.

JUDGES XIV. 18. 23

And the men of the city said unto him on the seventh day, before the [sun] went down, What is sweeter than honey? and what is stronger than a [lion] And he said unto them, If ye had not [ploughed] ye had not found out my riddle. with my [heifer]

And the men of the city said unto him on the seventh day, before the *sun* went down, What is sweeter than honey? and what is stronger than a *lion?* And he said unto them, If ye had not *ploughed* with my *heifer*, ye had not found out my riddle.

12

The significance of riddles and their impact on the culture of their times is perhaps best illustrated by the tragic results of a riddling match that occurred between Samson and the Philistines at his wedding feast.

It was Samson's intention to impress his wife's people with his brilliance by posing a riddle to them based on an unusual sight he had once seen, a swarm of bees making honey in the carcass of a lion. "Out of the eater came forth meat and out of the strong came forth sweetness," he propounded. So positive was he of the Philistines' inability to solve the riddle that he generously allowed them seven days to figure out the answer, promising a reward of thirty changes of clothing should they come up with the correct solution. It would have been impossible for the Philistines to solve this riddle, so closely was it based on an experience witnessed only by Samson. However, by threatening his wife with physical harm, they got her to entice the answer out of her husband and she passed it along to them. "What is sweeter than honey and what is stronger than a lion?" they smugly recited when the puzzlers reconvened the next week.

Hell hath no fury like a puzzlist scorned! Samson exploded, and his wrath set off a series of violent battles between him and the Philistines during which he lost his wife, killed thousands of Philistines, burned their corn fields and almost died of thirst. This is definitely the most bloody case of puzzling on record, where a riddle was directly responsible for divorce, despair and destruction.

The tragic riddling experiences of Samson and Oedipus were the exception rather than the rule with the ancients. Riddles were a diversion of kings and their courts and provided a principal form of entertainment for the cultivated populace. It was two kings, in fact, Solomon and Hiram, who were the principal players in the first recorded organized riddle contests. The two kings were to try to outwit each other with unsolvable riddles; the loser was to be fined when he couldn't figure out an answer. Initially, Solomon collected large sums of money from Hiram. However, the substitution of Abdemon for Hiram in subsequent contests caused a reversal in the balance of payments, and Solomon was ultimately the loser. Nonetheless, his reputation as a great riddler remained intact for it is further recorded that the Queen of Sheba journeyed forth especially to meet him to "prove him with hard questions" (I Kings 10:1).

The ancient Greeks were also fond of riddles. Enigmatical questions were special features at banquets and skill in riddling was regarded as proof of a good education. It is said that Cleopulus earned his title as one of the Seven Wise Men of Greece by authoring what is now known as "The Year Riddle":

13

"A father had twelve children and each child had thirty sons and daughters, the sons being white and the daughters black and one of them died every day and yet became immortal."

Riddle solving was so intertwined with one's reputation as an intellectual that some people equated inability to solve a puzzle with a loss of prestige. The fishermen of Ios challenged Homer with the following riddle: "What we caught we threw away, what we could not catch we kept." The answer, "fleas," eluded the great classical poet and so enraged him that he died of pique.

The ancient Romans, in their emulation of the Greek way of life, also embraced riddling as a popular form of entertainment. The Saturnalia, a religious festival akin to our Christmas, was an ideal time for riddles. When the gifts had been exchanged, the primary after-dinner recreation consisted of riddle posing and solving. As an added attraction, some hosts distributed party favors in the form of tickets upon which were written riddles describing the presents.

Riddles also appeared as inscriptions on tombstones. One wonders if this method was a means of revenge toward those still alive or merely a clever way to engrave a tombstone.

Why were riddles so highly regarded by the cultured classes in antiquity? Aristotle believed their appeal lay in their metaphorical quality. All riddles involve an element of deception; once the solver recognizes this connection between the riddle and its answer she or he could derive great satisfaction from having worked out the solution.

All the early riddles were in the form of enigmatical questions or conundrums posed verbally by riddlers to solvers primarily at games and feasts. Riddling took on a different aspect in the third to fourth century A.D. when a series of one hundred riddles appeared written in Latin hexameter three-line poems. The author of these riddles was Symphosius, an enigmatical fellow (no pun intended) about whom little is known. It is surmised that he was a non-Christian for no trace of Christianity appears in any of his riddles.

All of his riddles were titled so one did not have to "guess" at a solution. Rather, the beauty lay in appreciating the metaphorical allusions to the title, as can be seen in the following examples:

Mother of Twins

More have I borne than one body ought.
Three souls did I have, all of which I
had within me: a pair departed, but the
third nearly perished too.

14

Mule

**Unlike my mother, in semblance different
from my father, of mingled race, a breed
unfit for progeny, of others am I born, and
none is born of me.**

Symphosius's riddles were so popular that for centuries poets and enigmatists indiscriminately copied his themes. His most prolific emulator was Aldhelm, a seventh-century English scholar and poet whose main work, *De Metris,* consisted of a series of one hundred riddles. Unlike Symphosius, however, Aldhelm was a devout Christian whose main purpose in riddling was to glorify God and his creations. His riddles were concerned with everyday topics—animals, plants, stars, furniture, household items—and by being pre-titled were designed to reveal rather than hide. Symphosius's influence is quite obvious:

Dog

**Long since, the holy power that made all things
So made me that my master's dangerous foes
I scatter. Bearing weapons in my jaws,
I soon decide fierce combats; yet I flee
Before the lashings of a little child.**

Woman in Labor with Twins

**Six eyes are mine; as many ears have I;
Fingers and toes twice thirty do I bear.
Of these, when forty from my flesh are torn,
Lo, then but twenty will remain to me.**

For the riddle constructor, the objects in his immediate world were the usual subjects to embellish in puzzles. Claret, a fourteenth-century Benedictine monk, decided to add a new twist to the art in the collection of 136 riddles for which he became famous. Included in this work are some so-called "obscene" riddles, whereby suggestive images are used to describe a totally innocent subject. The riddles were so designed as to throw solvers completely off the track and lead them to something totally different (some would say "obscene"):

**A vessel have I
That is round like a pear,
Moist in the middle,
Surrounded with hair;
And often it happens
That water flows there.**

A vivid imagination will no doubt think of something else, but "eye" is the intended solution here!

Anagrams

Anagrams are an ancient form of word juggling. Their origin is ascribed to a Greek poet, Lycophron, who flourished in the fourth century B.C. King Ptolemy Philadelphus brought Lycophron to Egypt where he amused the king's court by wittily anagramming their names into less-than-flattering phrases. The poet knew his place, however. Recognizing the power of the throne, Lycophron cleverly transposed the Greek version of the king's name into a phrase that meant "made of honey," suggesting the sweetness of the ruler. He was equally flattering to the queen with her anagram—"violet of Juno."

Anagram devotees had great faith in the prophetic nature of anagrams and truly believed that the transposal of a name or word revealed one's destiny. This viewpoint is evidenced by an anagram which figured prominently in Alexander the Great's life. During the siege of Tyre, Alexander had qualms about his ability to conquer that city. He slept fitfully the night before the battle and dreamed that a satyr emerged from the woods and danced before him. He caught the satyr and then awoke. When his soothsayers were summoned to interpret the dream, they revealed that SATYR could be anagrammatized into TYRE IS THINE. Was this clairvoyance, or did the prophecy simply give Alexander the confidence he needed to win? No one can be sure, but next day the anagram came true. Plato, it is said, was also a believer in this form of augury.

One of the most famous anagrams of all was constructed during the Middle Ages. The author invented a dialogue between Pilate and Jesus whereby Pilate questions, "*Quid est veritas?*" (What is truth?) and Jesus replies, "*Est vir qui adest*" (It is the man before you.)

Anagrams did not really become popular until the thirteenth century when the Jewish Cabalists, in their quest to understand man's relationship to God, attached a mystical significance to numbers and letters of the alphabet. Anagramming was incorporated into their ways and then spread rapidly throughout the scholarly world to the cultivated of all nations.

Oftentimes an anagram became an excuse for a person to devote his life's work to a specific occupation. So pervasive was the belief in a mystical connection between objects and persons and their names that when André Pujon, a Frenchman, realized that his name could be transposed into "Pendu à Rion," he committed murder so he could be hanged at Rion, a local seat of criminal justice.

Anagrams were also popular with writers wishing to write under pen names. Voltaire's given name was Arouet, l.j. (*le jeune,* the younger). By substituting V for U and I for J (a com-

mon typographical practice in days of yore), he achieved his famous name. Calvinus was the pen name of Alcuinus and François Rabelais became Alcofribas Nasier.

The epitome of anagramming was believed to occur when the transposal of a name was directly related to the person's achievement or destiny in life. In this respect *Honor est a Nilo* (His honor comes from the Nile) was a perfect anagram for Horatio Nelson. It was coined by an English clergyman after Admiral Nelson's victory in Egypt.

Anagrams have also been constructed retrospectively to explain a person's fate in life. Had Mary, Queen of Scots, known what the anagram of her name revealed, perhaps she could have averted her tragic fate. Maria Steuarda Scotorum Regina, the Latin version of her name, when anagrammatized becomes *Trusa vi regnis morte amara cada*—Thrust by force from my kingdom I fall by a foul death.

17

An example of
Egyptian hiero-
glyphics from the
tomb of Ramose.
This ancient form of
picture writing was
the inspiration for
all heraldic devices
and rebus puzzles.

The Rebus

The rebus is the most visual puzzle variety. It derives from
hieroglyphics, a script composed of picture-like symbols devised
by the ancient Egyptians. Originally hieroglyphic writing inscribed in monuments could only be read by priests and other
learned people — it was a way of confining knowledge to a select
group of people.

Rebus coins inscribed with pictures representing famous people or their cities were popular in ancient Greece and Rome.
Julius Caesar's coins were imprinted with elephants, for that
was the translation of his name in the Mauritanian language.
Similarly, a rose for Rhodes and pomegranate for Melos were
equally representative.

Rebuses were very much in evidence during the Middle Ages
as decorations for heraldic devices. Heraldry was a system
through which families and dynasties could chronicle their exploits. Every birth, death, marriage and territorial acquisition
was faithfully depicted in the heraldic family arms and became
a *cause célèbre* for altering the coat of arms. In essence, these
shields became a concise pictorial history of the family.

OPPOSITE Heraldic
symbols were used
on badges, helmets,
crests, coats of arms
and other devices as
graphic representa-
tions of family
names and dynas-
ties. The many vari-
eties of trees and
leaves on these
shields show how
specific and unique
these pictures could
be.

It wasn't until the early seventeenth century that rebuses
reached the masses via the priests in the Picardy region of
France. Every year, during elaborate preparations for the great
Easter carnival, the priests would issue religious pamphlets
composed of words and pictures, so even the illiterate masses
would understand something of their message. The populace
embraced rebuses with a passion that bordered almost on
madness. Wealthy people made up pictorial versions of their
names, such as three castles for Castleton; towns adopted pun-
ning representations, such as rats for Arras and lion for Lyons;
book publishers used symbols for their logos, such as a pike

1. Oak Tree.
Wood.

2. Fir Tree.
M'Gregor.

3. Palm Tree.
Tagliavia.

4. Crequier.
Crequy.

5. Forest.
Busch.

6. Lime Branch.
Seckendorf.

7. Hazel Leaves.
Hazlerigg.

8. Laurel Leaves.
Foulis.

9. Lime Leaves adossés.
Ortlieb.

10. Trefoil.
Hervey.

11. Treflé.
Hilinger.

12. Quatrefoil.
Vincent.

The Lord God planted a

in Eden; and there he put the man, to dress it, and to keep it; saying, Thou mayest freely eat of all the

of the garden;

but of the

of the knowledge of good and evil, thou shalt not eat of it: for in the day that thou eatest thereof thou shalt surely die.

The Lord God planted a *garden* in Eden; and there he put the man, to dress it, and to keep it; saying, Thou mayest freely eat of all the *trees* of the garden; but of the *tree* of the knowledge of good and evil, thou shalt not eat of it: for in the day that thou eatest thereof thou shalt surely die.

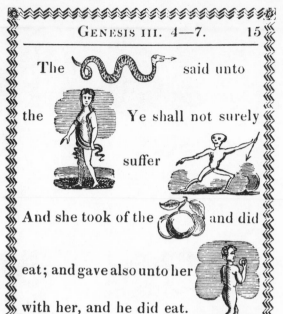

The [serpent] said unto the [woman], Ye shall not surely suffer [death]. And she took of the [fruit], and did eat; and gave also unto her [husband] with her, and he did eat. And their [eyes] were opened, and they knew that they were naked.

The serpent *said unto the* woman, *Ye shall not surely suffer* death. *And she took of the* fruit, *and did eat; and gave also unto her* husband *with her, and he did eat. And their* eyes *were opened, and they knew that they were naked.*

A "Puzzler's Paradise" before the Fall—passages from a nineteenth-century hieroglyphic Bible, similar to the example shown on p. 12.

through a ring for Pickering or a hare, rye and sun for Harrison.

Rebuses today are mainly found in children's puzzle books. The first places for children's picture puzzles were early hieroglyphical Bibles. It was assumed that children, like the illiterate masses in Picardy, would be able to learn their lessons in "a delightful manner" through such Bibles.

Cryptography

Cryptography, or code writing, is another form of puzzling, albeit a more serious one, for interpreting messages between sender and receiver. There are examples of coded words in the Bible; the Romans and Greeks were known to use cryptographs and sometimes secret messages were transmitted through writings on slaves' heads.

Ciphers were especially valuable during war time, enabling couriers to transmit messages that couldn't be deciphered by the enemy. Great military minds were often well versed in cryptography. One of the most dramatic unintentional ciphers was an inscription made by Darius the Great on the Behistun Rock in Iran 2,500 years ago. So pleased was he with his military exploits that he flaunted his strategical tactics in a trilingual message. It literally took centuries for modern man to break the "code," but when scholars did finally interpret the ancient writing it provided the key to all cuneiform writing of the past.

Other ciphers have eluded interpretation for long periods of time. Rabanus Maurus, a ninth-century archbishop who was one of the most learned men of his time, left a ciphered message which wasn't translated until centuries after his death. His forte consisted of inscribing messages in diagrams against a backdrop of extraneous letters. Only the letters within the heavy black lines were meaningful and when rearranged formed the message.

Picturesque puzzling by Rabanus Maurus. The ninth-century archbishop drew symbolic figures containing a scrambled coded message against a background of extraneous letters.

Palindromes and Magic Word Squares

Palindromes are sentences which read the same backwards and forwards. Some scholars have wittily suggested that Adam's first words to Eve might have been "Madam, I'm Adam"—a perfectly appropriate palindromic introduction which no doubt would have dazzled the First Lady. An ancient Roman palindrome popular with lawyers was *"Si nummi immunis"*—If you pay you will go free. A famous palindrome "Lewd did I live & evil I did dwel" contained some imperfections (use of the ampersand and an old spelling of dwell) yet has also been handed down to us—an indication of not only the cleverness of the puzzle, but perhaps its universality as well!

An important ingredient affecting the life span of a puzzle is its degree of unsolvability. Generally those puzzles which proved to be especially difficult for would-be solvers when they were first constructed have been passed down through the ages. In terms of elusiveness one of the most famous puzzles of all is the Sator Acrostic, an unusual word square that was found during an excavation on the site of the Roman city of Cirencester in England. It appears to have been written upon the wall of a room as follows:

R O T A S

O P E R A

T E N E T

A R E P O

S A T O R

Its uniqueness lies in the fact that it can be read both backwards and forwards and is thus a palindromic word square—a fact which eluded scholars for years. A generally accepted translation of the acrostic words is "Arepo, the sower, carefully guides the wheels," which loosely means God controls the universe. However, opinions are varied and voluminous as to how the word square was actually used. One suggestion was that it was worn as an amulet to ward off bites from rabid animals. Another, that it was used as a toothache cure: the letters would be written on pieces of bread and butter and then swallowed; by digesting the magic words the sickness would be expelled. Still others had it that it was used to extinguish fires or as a charm against fever, or that because it is a palindrome, it served a dual purpose—by reading the puzzle forwards one could call up the spirits and when read backwards they would be banished again.

Magic squares did exist in ancient times but they were

The Sator Acrostic, the palindromic word square found in Cirencester, England, in 1868.

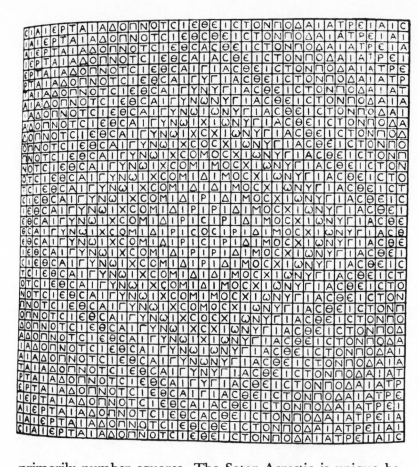

Moschion's word square tribute to Osiris was inscribed in an alabaster slab. This use of letters in squares to form words horizontally and vertically is believed by some scholars to be an integral link to the crossword.

primarily number squares. The Sator Acrostic is unique because it is the only word square to come down to us from antiquity, and if the foregoing scholarly dispute is any indication it will undoubtedly remain one of the great "puzzles" of all times.

Another interesting and more elaborate word square is the stele of Moschion. This 39 × 39 square, incised in alabaster, was found in Egypt and dates from the second or third century A.D. To read this puzzle start at the center 0 and read right or left, up or down, to the end and then turn at right angles to the next corner. The same phrase, "Moschion to Osiris, for the treatment which cured his foot," is repeated over and over again. This was evidently devised as a tribute to the god Osiris for healing Moschion's foot—a clever and intricate example of the lengths to which people would go to please their gods.

No chapter on puzzle origins would be complete without mention of King David's alphabetic acrostic. In Psalm 119 each eight-line stanza begins with words whose initials are the letters of the Hebrew alphabet in order (aleph, beth, gimel and so on). Known as the Abecedarian Psalm, it is perhaps the earliest known form of the acrostic.

❯COMING OF AGE❮

The puzzles from antiquity which have survived through the ages owe their immortality to their uniqueness. Worthy of being remembered and repeated, they were passed along verbally, from generation to generation. How many hundreds of thousands of puzzles must have passed into oblivion over the centuries!

Since the advent of printing, however, much has changed. Puzzles began to crop up in books and magazines, and their popularity grew at an amazing rate. And since the advent of mass publishing, a voluminous number of puzzles have been retained. A study of these puzzles shows a remarkable parallel to the growth of literature. Puzzles in the sixteenth through nineteenth centuries were considered artistic manifestations of the creative mind and were sometimes seen to rival the best literary works of the times. Many famous poets and philosophers constructed puzzles and brought to them those same creative powers that they used in their accustomed literary and intellectual pursuits. An entirely different outlook exists today. Puzzle solvers view their hobby as an amusing and somewhat educational way to pass the time. Puzzle constructors, while serious about their products, rarely equate their output with artistic expression.

This evolution of puzzles from an art form to an amusing recreation took place over several centuries and is closely intertwined with the overall development of the western world. Influencing the shift, among other things, were the change from an agricultural to an industrial society; the emergence of the literate masses; the reduction of the work week; the growing emphasis on leisure-time activities; the introduction of movies and television; and the resulting competition for people's time between visual media and the written word.

By looking at selected puzzles in relation to their literary and historical milieus, modern puzzlers can see for the first time the relationship of puzzles to the cultural growth of the world, and by so doing, truly deepen their appreciation of puzzling as the oldest recreational pastime.

The earliest written puzzles in America appeared in a 1647

almanac published by Samuel Danforth, a printer who had emigrated from England and graduated from Harvard. His almanac contained the usual astronomical and astrological data and, as an added attraction, a series of twelve original enigmatical verses, one for each month. Most of Danforth's riddles were concerned with the day-to-day realities of life in colonial America. This one, for July, is typical of the metaphorical allusions used so often in verses of this type:

> The wooden Birds are now in sight,
> Whose voices roare, whose wings are white,
> Whose mawes are fill'd with hose and shoes,
> With wine, cloth, sugar, salt and newes,
> When they have eas'd their stomacks here
> They cry, farewell until next yeare.

The "wooden Birds," of course, refer to the ships bringing supplies to the colonists.

It is a tribute to the creative process embedded within each of us that any poetry appeared at all in the early colonial days. Conditions in seventeenth-century New England were

A pince-nezed politician perilously perusing his evening paper. Perhaps it's the puzzle page that has him so painfully preoccupied.

25

hardly conducive to literary pursuits. Almanacs were the most logical place for puzzles to gain popularity as most colonists' libraries, such as they were, contained only a Bible and an almanac. Puzzles similar to Danforth's thus began to appear in other almanacs of the time and served as one of the few popular entertainments the struggling early colonists allowed themselves.

In seventeenth-century England, where conditions were more advanced, books of puzzles were already being printed. In fact, a book of riddles had been printed prior to 1575 and was mentioned in Shakespeare's *The Merry Wives of Windsor*. Books of riddles were popular among all classes of people. Published in 1629, *The Merry Book of Riddles,* contained some interesting examples of the classical-allusion type of riddle as the following points out:

> **He went to the wood and caught it,**
> **He sate him downe and sought it;**
> **Because he could not finde it,**
> **Home with him he brought it.**

The solution was extensively embellished:

> **That is a thorne: for a man went to the wood, and caught a thorne in his foote, and then he sate him down, and sought to have it pulled out, and because he could not find it out, he must needs bring it home.**

King Louis XIII of France was even further along than his English brethren in his pursuit of leisure-time activities. Puzzling was a favorite pastime of his, and he embraced it in a grand manner. He employed a gentleman by the name of Thomas Billon as his "Royal Anagrammatist." This fellow received a salary and ranked as high as any of the poet laureates of the time. It is difficult to judge how creative he was as none of his anagrams have come down to us, but he does occupy a unique place in puzzle history.

Riddles in the eighteenth century became more sophisticated and there are some striking examples of very finely constructed puzzles. In addition, new puzzle types were being invented. In England, where puzzles had already made their impact on the populace, puzzle columns had become a regular feature of many periodicals. The following puzzle, from such a column, involved the building up of words from syllabic clues and was actually a prelude to the charade, a form which became immensely popular during the late 1700s:

> **From the Mate of the Cock, Winter-Corn in the Ground,**
> **The Christian Name of my Friend may be found:**
> **Join the song of a cat, to the Place Hermits dwell in,**
> **Gives the sirname of him who does Musick excell in.**

King Louis XIII, prince of puzzling.

The explanation was as follows:

Here the Mate of a Cock is a HEN: THE WINTER-CORN is either
WHEAT or RYE; but because it is to make up a Name, it is the
latter is meant: So the Christian Name is HENRY. Then the
Song of a Cat is what we call the PUR of a Cat; and the Place a
Hermit dwells in is call'd a CELL so the sirname is PURCELL: SO
THAT THIS REBUS IS UPON THE NAME of M. HENRY PURCELL, the late
famous Master of Musick, perhaps the best that ever
ENGLAND bred.

Henry Purcell, master
of music.

On both sides of the Atlantic, puzzles were popular with
many intellectuals of the period. Writers, poets, philosophers
and statesmen, known for their more literary works, composed
and solved enigmas and riddles for their own amusement.

Benjamin Franklin composed some interesting riddles for his
Poor Richard's Almanack of 1736. The difference between his
enigmas and Danforth's show how the growing sophistication of
a young nation could influence puzzle constructors. Franklin's
"enigmatical prophecies" were sometimes elusive to readers,
who, when unable to figure out the answer, had to wait until
the following year before satisfying their curiosity. It must have
been a bit alarming to have the following riddle puzzle you for
365 days (especially if you believed in the prophetic nature of
the riddle!):

Not long after (the middle of the Year), a visible Army of
20,000 Musketers will land, some in Virginia and Maryland,
and some in the lower Counties on both sides of Delaware,
who will over-run the Country, and sorely annoy the Inhabitants: But the Air in this Climate will agree with them so ill
towards Winter, that they will die in the beginning of cold
weather like rotten Sheep, and by Christmas the Inhabitants
will get the better of them.

Almanac readers were relieved to learn the following year that:

The Army which it was said would land in Virginia, Maryland,
and the Lower Counties of Delaware, were not Musketers
with Guns on their Shoulders as some expected; but their
Namesakes, in Pronunciation, tho' truly spelt Moschitos,
arm'd only with a sharp sting. Every one knows they are Fish
before they fly, being bred in the Water; and therefore may
properly be said to land before they become generally
troublesome.

In France, Voltaire, when he wasn't composing poetry or
writing philsophical treatises, managed to compose some enigmas that are as apropos today as they were in the eighteenth
century. Here is one of his most famous:

27

What of all things in the world is the longest, the shortest, the swiftest, the slowest, the most divisible and most extended, most regretted, most neglected, without which nothing can be done, and with which many do nothing, which destroys all that is little and ennobles all that is great?

Time

Horatio Walpole, the English politician and man of letters, included three enigmas in his *Works*. One of them is especially creative:

> **Before my birth I had a name,**
> **But soon as born I chang'd the same;**
> **And when I'm laid within the tomb,**
> **I shall my father's name assume.**
> **I change my name three days together**
> **Yet live but one in any weather.**

Today

It was during the eighteenth century that mass-marketed publications were introduced to the American public. One of the first periodicals to be more than a short-lived venture was *The American Magazine and Historical Chronicle*. In the very first issue a puzzle "for the ladies" appeared, a rather elaborate riddle about a needle, which by today's standards would appear to be overdone. One verse will suffice to indicate how important the author judged this instrument to be in the lives of women:

> **When wicked men their wealth consume,**
> **And leave their children poor,**
> **To me their daughters often come,**
> **And I increase their store.**

With the advent of an appropriate literary milieu, the magazine, new puzzle types began to appear. The charade was introduced in America in *The Penny Post,* a Philadelphia magazine published in 1769. While some of the charades published therein were of mediocre quality, it is significant that the magazine editors felt that the public was ready to accept new puzzle forms. One of the first charades appears below; although no answer was ever printed, the suggested answer, Maidstone, a small English town, points to the possibility that this puzzle must have been copied from a British source:

> **Take a word which is us'd to express a young lass.**
> **A material which building contains.**
> **A town you'll discover or I am an ass.**
> **And you are a dunce for your pains.**

Passionate times were sometimes propitious in terms of spurring on puzzle developments. The American Revolution, for example, spawned two famous rebuses which were vehicles of political satire. Matthew Darly, a British engraver, published these two rebuses in 1778, one from "Britannia to America" and the other from "America to her Mistaken Mother." In the first (see p. 30) England implored her headstrong daughter to reconsider her intentions of aligning with the French and implored America not to rebel. The American response indicated the determination of the colonists to achieve their independence. The rebuses were published prior to the British-sponsored peace attempts and prophesied the colonist's refusal to meet with the Carlisle Commission, the negotiating group appointed by King George III.

In America, the period after the Revolutionary War was a time of growth for literary and intellectual pursuits. Innovative puzzle types were introduced to receptive audiences as scores of new magazines and newspapers came into being. One variety that achieved popularity during this time was the acrostic rebus. In this type of puzzle, clues were presented in verse form (usually one clue per line), and the initial letters of each word would spell out a final word or name. The following acrostic is taken from *The Gentleman and Lady's Town and Country Magazine* of 1784:

> **A thing whereon all Princes lie**
> **And as we all express a sigh,**
> **What man into the world brings in**
> **An Indian weed whose leaf is thin;**
> **A wood by Kings esteemed much**
> **The part of speech when naming such:**
> **These initials join'd declare**
> **A town where friendly people are.**

The first letters of the clued words, **B**ed, **O**h, **S**in, **T**obacco, **O**ak, **N**oun, spell out the answer, BOSTON, the name of the town where the magazine was published.

Puzzles in the late 1700s were extremely popular and appeared frequently in literary, women's and family magazines. The number of people sending in puzzle solutions to magazines was surprisingly high for an era when letter writing was rather uncommon—a sure indication of the popularity puzzles had achieved. Puzzle solving was much more pronounced among the women of that period than among the men. Enigmas were often addressed specifically "to the ladies." A female reader, writing to the editor of *Boston Magazine* in 1784, told of the appeal of puzzles to members of her sex:

> **It is well known that our sex have long been the admirers and framers of enigmas. No part of the production, believe me, has been more read and applauded. I visit in almost every family in town, genteel and vulgar, and from Lady — down**

OVERLEAF "Britannia to America," one of the two famous political rebuses executed by Matthew Darly on the eve of the American Revolution. The second, "America to her mistaken mother," was an equally clever pictorial reply in which the "greatly injured Daughter Amerik" responded caustically: "guard well your own triflings & leave me to myself as I am at an age to know my own interests without your foolish advice . . . ." (See Picture Answers, 1.)

29

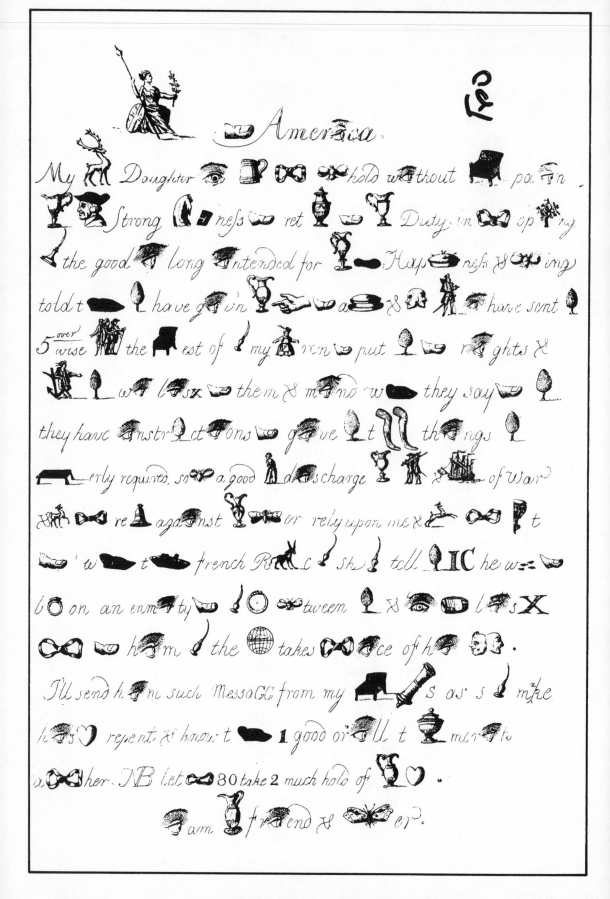

to Dorothy my maid, every female understanding has been exercised in the discovery of those which you have published.

Puzzles involving letter manipulation were starting to become popular during the latter part of the eighteenth century. Beheadments and transpositions were two puzzle types introduced at this time. In a beheadment, a versified clue is given for two words, the second of which is missing the initial letter of the first. In a transposition, the answer consists of two words containing the same letters but spelling entirely different words. Here is a typical beheadment:

> **Children detest me oft' at school,**
> **Because I give them many a rule;**
> **Take the first letter from my name,**
> **And you will every soldier blame,**
> **If he on guard should dare appear,**
> **Without he has me very near.** *Marms-Arms*

The earliest transpositions usually involved short words. Again, here is a typical example:

> **An insect of the smallest kind**
> **If you transpose, you soon will find**
> **That from all mortals I do quickly fly;**
> **When gone, my loss in vain they'll mourn**
> **In vain will wish for my return.**
> **Tho' now to kill me, ev'ry art they try.** *Mite-Time*

The first American book devoted exclusively to puzzles was published in 1787, and it was enthusiastically accepted. *The Little Puzzling Cap*, as it was titled, contained a series of riddles based on familiar objects, such as scissors, a pair of spectacles

BELOW An 1805 variation on *The Little Puzzle Cap*. Note the publisher. John Adams, second president of the United States (1797-1801), was said to be interested in puzzles, but whether this is his imprint is a matter of speculation. Riddle books such as this were meant to be read aloud. The picture was always included so the reciter could know the answer while reading the rhyme to the listener.

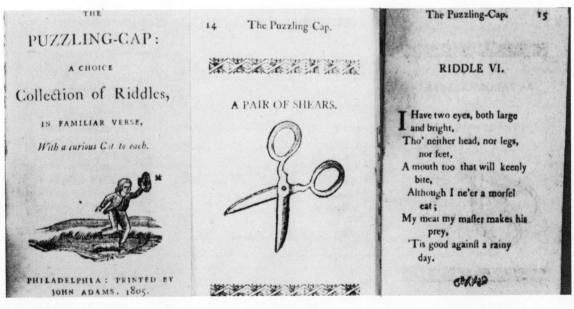

THE
PUZZLING-CAP:
A CHOICE
Collection of Riddles,
IN FAMILIAR VERSE,
With a curious Cut to each.

PHILADELPHIA: PRINTED BY
JOHN ADAMS. 1805.

14   The Puzzling Cap.

A PAIR OF SHEARS.

The Puzzling-Cap.   15

RIDDLE VI.

I Have two eyes, both large
and bright,
Tho' neither head, nor legs,
nor feet,
A mouth too that will keenly
bite,
Although I ne'er a morsel
eat;
My meat my master makes his
prey,
'Tis good against a rainy
day.

and a water pot. Due to nonexistent copyright laws, new versions of this book were printed in various cities over the next twenty years. While some of the original riddles were dropped and new ones added, the core of the book remained the same. Essentially all the different printers had the same intention of gearing the book to a mass audience. The riddles contained pictures of the subject matter along with an enigmatical poem describing the object in paradoxical terms.

It is conceivable that this book was copied from a riddle book that first appeared in England, Scotland and Ireland in 1778. The collection was authored by "John-the-Giant-Killer" and contained puzzles such as the following:

NO twins could e'er with us com
pare,
So like in ſhape and ſize ;
Our bodies are like ermin fair
As black as jet our eyes :
But tho' ſo like in ev'ry feature,
We rival brothers be ;
Yet ſo obdurate is our nature,
We often diſagree.

A pair of dice

32

Some puzzle books were authored by popular writers under noms-de-plume. Pen names were used because not everybody viewed puzzle construction as a worthy pastime, and the literati feared that their reputations might suffer should it be discovered that they were involved in frivolous pursuits. Nonetheless, enough puzzle constructors were proud to affix their signatures to their creations so that these pen-name puzzlers were in the minority.

As a culture shifts its emphasis from agriculture to industry, the literary forms which served to entertain in the past no longer remain acceptable. Literature, among other cultural and social institutions, must adapt to the new society's needs or risk obsolescence. During the accelerated growth period of the nineteenth century, many innovations were introduced in puzzling to allow it to remain a palatable pastime. Along the way many puzzle aficionados were made.

Among the people whose interest in puzzles grew during this period were the residents of rural areas. In America in 1802 the widely circulated *Farmer's Almanack* began to include enigmas in the poetry and anecdotes section. These must have been well received for each subsequent almanac contained puzzles. As in all almanacs, readers had a one-year period to figure out the answer to puzzles, such as this first enigma:

Before creating Nature will'd
 That atoms into form should jar,
By me the boundless space was fill'd
 On me was hung the first-made star.
For me the saint will break his word;
 By the proud atheist I'm rever'd;
At me the coward draws his sword,
 And by the hero I am fear'd.
Scorned by the meek and humble mind,
 Yet often by the vain possess'd,
Heard by the deaf, seen by the blind,
 And to the troubled conscience rest.
Than Wisdom's sacred self I'm wiser,
 And yet by every blockhead known;
I'm freely given by the miser,
 Kept by the prodigal alone.
As vice deform'd, as virtue fair,
 The courtier's loss, the patriot's gains.
The poet's purse, the coxcomb's care;
 Read and you'll have me for your pains.

The following year this succinct line appeared: "Nothing will best answer the riddle in last year's almanack."

Puzzles in almanacs and rural magazines were embraced warmly by farm folks because their educational level was on the rise and they were becoming attracted to intellectual amusements. Furthermore, farm life was conducive to the study of puzzles for families were forced to spend a great deal of time indoors during the long winter months and recreations of all types were welcomed.

A significant development in puzzling's metamorphosis from a literary manifestation to a recreational amusement in America was the introduction of puzzle columns in magazines. Some of the very first columns appeared sporadically in the early 1800s in such magazines as *The Lady's Monitor* and *New York Weekly Museum* and featured simple, yet clever charades such as the following:

> **My *first* is what the married wish,**
> **And happiness imparts to Lords;**
> **My *next* takes captive many a fish,**
> **My *whole* amusement oft affords.**

Sonnet

Although none of the earliest puzzle columns lasted any appreciable length of time, their appearance is evidence that editors wanted to make puzzles a regular feature of their magazines.

As the century progressed, more diverse types of publications, such as magazines and newspapers in both urban and rural areas, started to include columns devoted exclusively to puzzles. Puzzles were rarely found in the poetry section of a publication, except, of course, in literary magazines. And as puzzles became more popular with the masses, poetic style began to be de-emphasized in favor of the puzzling element.

A charade taken from "The Enigmas" column in *The Minerva* magazine of the 1820s shows the simple style then being used by constructors. Although the puzzle is written in verse, it is by no means as esoteric as some of its earlier counterparts:

> **My first you will be,**
> **If you're good and upright:**
> **My second you'll see**
> **In a sharp frosty night.**
> **Together combined,**
> **I'm a virtue that's great,**
> **That should govern each mind,**
> **And preside in each state.**

Justice

Puzzle columns began to appear in children's magazines as well. *Our Young Folks,* a widely circulated magazine, contained an ambitious puzzle column which lasted about ten years. Called "Round the Evening Lamp," this feature was

ILLUSTRATED REBUS.—No. 4

ENIGMAS.

NO. 3.

I am composed of 16 letters.

My 3, 15, 4, 10, the poor need this winter.

My 4, 9, 7, 11, 14, 16, most of you will be next summer.

My 1, 2, 6, 11, was the first rebel.

My 3, 12, 5, 1, 14, the Copperheads want.

My 8, 12, 13, 1, 10, the Rebels will soon beg for.

My whole is the name of one of the contributors to "Our Young Folks."

A. O. W.

NO. 4.

I am composed of 19 letters.

My 5, 14, 13, 19, 18, 14, is very hard.

My 16, 2, 15, 9, 3, 18, 19, was best known in the Inquisition.

My 4, 11, 12, 5, is a French coin.

My 16, 12, 15, 8, 11, 13, 19, 18, is often baked for good children.

My 8, 17, 9, is something that squirrels appreciate.

My 4, 8, 6, 18, 19, we should avoid.

My 1, 15, 6, 7, 10, you can trace an Indian by.

My 10, 14, 8, 16, is a time when much fish is sold.

My 15, 19, 13, 14, 18, 14, is what every loyal citizen does for the Union.

My 5, 8, 7, 13, 14, 10, is what cowards do.

My 4, 6, 7, 8, 1, is an excellent person.

My 14, 6, 4, 9, is in the neighborhood of sunrise.

My whole is the name of a hero, contemporary with Napoleon Bonaparte.

ARITHMETICAL PUZZLES.

NO. 6.

Take just one half of forty-one,
And when you think 't is rightly done
Add twenty-one, and, sure as fate,
The sum will be just twenty-eight.

NO. 7.

To six perpendicular lines add five, and get nine for a result.

J. T. S.

ILLUSTRATED REBUS.—No. 5.

(NAMES OF ENGLISH AUTHORS.)

packed with diverse puzzles such as charades, rebuses, enigmas and arithmetical puzzles and could literally amuse children for hours. A major advance in word puzzling occurred when puzzle books for adults were published. The first American one, in 1806, was composed of enigmas, rebuses and charades "designed for the improvement of the fair sex." It was called *The New American Oracle; or Ladies' Companion* and in view of the popularity of puzzles with the distaff sex seemed an appropriate premiere book. Its purpose was to elevate the level of puzzles presented to women. Here is a beheadment from it, which dealt with an extremely sensitive subject and with just a slight modernization of the language would be equally valid today:

> **In many countries I'm produc'd,**
> **And am to man a blessing:**
> **But blessings, when they are abus'd,**
> **A curse prove in possessing.**
> **There liv'd a race of men on earth**
> **With nature not contented,**
> **From them did art derive her birth,**
> **In various shapes invented;**
> **'Mong those, the art to drain my blood,**
> **Was held in veneration,**
> **And deem'd to be extremely good,**
> **In almost ev'ry nation.**
> **The bucks and rakes, and such like breed,**
> **And each audacious varlet,**
> **When they can get it, they'll exceed**
> **The babylonish harlot;**
> **Then ladies, would you know the crime**
> **They're capable of doing,**
> **One letter taken from my name,**
> **Will shew it to your viewing:**
> **But justice soon pursues the rake,**
> **'Fore whom they stand and tremble,**
> **Then from my name two letters take,**
> **You'll see what they resemble.**

Grape-Rape-Ape

The second puzzle book, published five years later, set the tone for the numerous puzzle books that appeared throughout the nineteenth century. The only thing unwieldy about the book was its title: *The Whim-Wham: or Evening Amusement, for All Ages and Sizes. Being an Entire New Set of Riddles, Charades, Questions and Transpositions.* However, the puzzles contained within were written mainly in simple, prose style. Directed at the average person, they were nowhere as literary as those in *The New American Oracle*. Here are two examples:

36

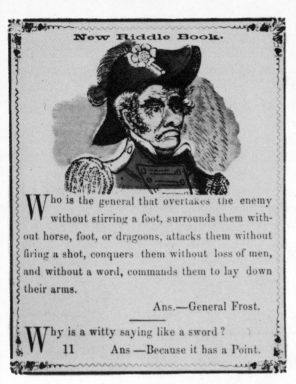

New Riddle Book.

Who is the general that overtakes the enemy without stirring a foot, surrounds them without horse, foot, or dragoons, attacks them without firing a shot, conquers them without loss of men, and without a word, commands them to lay down their arms.

Ans.—General Frost.

Why is a witty saying like a sword?
11   Ans —Because it has a Point.

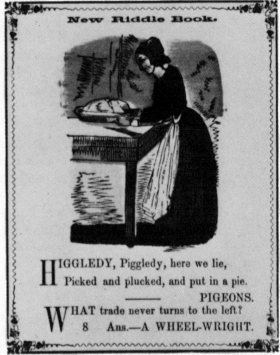

New Riddle Book.

Higgledy, Piggledy, here we lie,
Picked and plucked, and put in a pie.
——   PIGEONS.
What trade never turns to the left?
8   Ans.—A WHEEL-WRIGHT.

I am taken from the mine: confin'd in a wooden case; and am used by many people.

My first is one of the elements; without my second we should be very helpless; and my whole should never be put in the hands of a madman.

Excerpts from a children's puzzle book. The answers are not readily apparent and definitely demanded some reasoning ability on the listener's part.

The answers, A PENCIL and FIREARMS respectively, were within reach of most readers.

Puzzle books proliferated during the nineteenth century. Specialty books, containing only one type of puzzle, were printed, primarily for children. One series, *The Illustrated Book of Riddles,* was printed in color, which was an innovation for that time. The riddles were meant to be read aloud by adults and were rather sophisticated. Sometimes puzzle books were privately printed and distributed only to friends and acquaintances because the author had received several requests for favorite puzzles. Other books, although privately financed, were sold to the public and the proceeds were then distributed to charitable organizations. Magazine editors gathered the cream of their puzzle columns and reproduced them in book form. Special occasions were sometimes propitious times for the printing and distribution of puzzle books, such as the volume *Original Charades Prepared for the Fair in Aid of the Bunker Hill Monument.*

The latter half of the nineteenth century was a turning point in American puzzle history, for it was during this period that puzzles really staked their claim as a permanent fixture in the leisure-time activity arena. The marketplace was literally inundated with puzzle books.

New and exciting puzzle types continued to be developed. Puzzle columns had begun to appear in a wide variety of magazines, and small publications devoted exclusively to puzzles began to spring up. The period also saw the formation of the first organized puzzling societies. Each of these trends was important by itself in stimulating more and more people to become puzzle devotees. However, the combination of them occurring simultaneously propelled puzzling into an established recreational amusement.

Some of the puzzles which became popular during this time were word squares, conundrums, picture and letter rebuses, double acrostics and numerical puzzles. The first six-letter word square in America, in which the same words read across and down, appeared in *Godey's Lady's Book and Magazine* in 1862. This puzzle had originally appeared in the English periodical *Notes and Queries* in 1859:

```
C  I  R  C  L  E

I  C  A  R  U  S

R  A  R  E  S  T

C  R  E  A  T  E

L  U  S  T  R  E

E  S  T  E  E  M
```

This was the beginning of form puzzles, which would eventually become the mainstay of all puzzles in the twentieth century.

Conundrums were like riddles only much more fun. The answer was always a pun or pleasant joke. Some books of conundrums contained the answers right next to the questions so there was no need to delay one's laughter, as in these examples:

Why is a lovely woman like ambition?
She steals (steels) the heart.

Plant a puppy and what would come up?
Dog would.

Why couldn't Eve have the measles?
She'd Adam (had 'em).

Did Jonah cry when the whale swallowed him?
He thought he was going to blubber, but he didn't.

Distribution presented a unique challenge to puzzle publishers. In the absence of a national medium to advertise, some

A scene from *Billy Black's Cabinet of Conundrums* showing the unique marketing system used by some puzzle book publishers. Vendors were employed to hawk the books in the streets.

publishers employed vendors to hawk their books in the street. The spiels were often lively and distinctive, particularly when it came to hawking books of conundrums. Other publishers were more traditional and advertised their puzzle books in magazines or on the back covers of other books.

Rebuses were often considered children's puzzles because of

Riddle books were also advertised via more traditional means, as seen in this ad by an English printer. The sales pitches were similar on both sides of the Atlantic.

their dependence on pictures. However, rebuses used in adult books were not necessarily juvenile, as witnessed in the preface to *Aunt Sue's Budget of Puzzles,* a collection of riddles, charades and enigmas, pictured on page 41.

A more advanced rebus was the letter type whereby the placement of letters and words in unique positions created a puzzle that was far from child's play. Two examples will suffice to show you how sophisticated and visually challenging these puzzles were:

To be

aaaaaaaaaa

t C r l i O f U l S e s

standing

is the mark of a mean

Look

Look   U   Look

Look

&

C that o VXS nor xx UR ii.

To be overtenacious in the midst of trifles is the mark of a mean understanding.

Look around you always and see that nothing vexes nor crosses your eyes.

PREFACE.

HE Enigma is of such ancient and RE able origin, t 🎩 👁 shall ask no 1 2 XQQ me 4 offering this 📖 2 the public. Enigmatical ?? R frequent the Scriptures, and olden times of 10 contained a deal of FVOARLMUAATBILOEN.

The preface to *Aunt Sue's Budget of Puzzles,* cast in an extremely clever rebus format. The author's defense of puzzles indicated that some people were still a trifle insecure about the role of puzzles in intellectual circles. (*See* Picture Answers, 3.)

This type of puzzle was often a perfect forum for moralistic preaching.

Double acrostics became immediately popular after their introduction in the mid-1860s. In this type of puzzle a number of words had to be guessed from definitions given, usually in verse form. The first and last initials of these words, reading downwards, spelled out the intended answer. In the example below, as in most acrostics, the horizontal words were not always the same length:

Perform my *first* with skill and care:
My *second,* then, I'll let you share,

1. When she learned the news that her lover she'd miss,
   She went to her room and could only do this.   W ee P

2. It isn't square, it isn't round,
   And yet between them 'twill be found.   O va L

3. In the kingdom of Italy it ever has been
   And out of its precincts it never is seen.   R avenn A

4. Without it, dogs you ne'er could muzzle,
   And 'tis the key to find this puzzle.   K e Y

Numerical word puzzles were of varied types and provided a change of pace. In the example below, a keyword was divided into its component letters, which were numbered consecutively. Clues were given using the various numbers and one had to figure out the whole word by assigning the correct letters to each number:

I am composed of 9 letters: my 4, 5, 6 is a full
amount; my 6, 5, 4, 8 is to think; my 3, 2, 1 is
indistinct; my 3, 9, 5, 6 is a musical instrument;
my 7, 8, 9 is French for sea; my 1, 2, 3 is
intervening; my whole is here now.

Midsummer

Although many puzzle books dealt exclusively with only one or two types of puzzles, others posed a wide variety of stumpers on every page, assuring that there was something for everyone no matter what his skills or interests.

Some of the most extensive puzzle columns were found in juvenile magazines. The editors used noms-de-plume and maintained a chatty correspondence with their young readers. The columns, bearing such names as "Puzzle Drawer" (found in *Merry's Museum*), "Round the Evening Lamp" (in *Our Young Folks*), and "Round Table" (in *Frank Leslie's Boys & Girls Weekly*), were enormously well received. Often an editor would capitalize on the following he developed from his magazine and publish a book of puzzles culled from its columns.

OPPOSITE A mélange of puzzles from an 1895 book shows how many diverse types of puzzles had reached the public by this time. Puzzle No. 446 is still a popular riddle with puzzlers today. (*See* Picture Answers, 4.)

such varying weights that by means of them a neighbouring groceryman was able to weigh articles of any integral weight from 1 to 40 pounds.

Required, the weights of the four pieces.

No. 444.—Conundrums.

When is a dog like a wandering minstrel?

Why is a buckwheat cake like a caterpillar?

Why is human life the riddle of all riddles?

Why does a duck go into the water?

Why is a quiet conscience like a fit of indigestion?

What is that which never asks questions yet requires many answers?

No. 445.—Charades.

(a) My first I may in truth declare—
Its name and nature both is air;
My second is a perfect bore,
Yet makes sweet music evermore;
My whole in many a crowded street
Lies in its bed beneath your feet.

(b) At evening by my whole you'll think
Of days gone by, and never reckon
That by my second my first is made,
And by my first my second.

No. 446.—A Picture Puzzle.

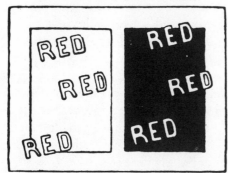

The above cut describes in seven words a very familiar object. What is the description and what is the object?

No. 447.—Numerical Enigma.

I am composed of 13 letters, and am a popular novelist of the day.

My 10, 3, 9 is a conveyance. My 12, 3, 13, 5 is to be conveyed. My 1, 11, 9 is an old woman. My 7, 5, 12, 5 is at this place. My 1, 5, 11, 4 is an important part of a man. My 6, 8, 2, 5 is precious. My 7, 11, 2, 13 is difficult to penetrate.

No. 448.—Articles of Furniture.

(a) A treatise and a box.

(b) To watch over, and a gown.

(c) A marsh and not to yield.

(d) Very, and a musical syllable.

No. 449.—A Geographical Acrostic.

(a) An Asiatic country.

(b) A Spanish river.

(c) An Italian river.

(d) A Russian province.

(e) An American territory.

(f) A Chinese city.

Initials and finals name two cities of Europe.

No. 450.—The Knight's Puzzle.

tle	to	a	cat-	life	and	live	In
By	tle	ow-	bro wse	of	non	tle	fall
ter	tur-	gain	like	land	one's	quiet	And
of	ar m	Bet-	me ad-	and	Than	a-	bat-
bask	Be t-	lau-	or	tle	ness	done	wan-
rel	let	Than	die	With	der	of	smo ke
ter	in	brain	myr-	on	and	har-	un-
Ch ap-	or	to	sun	with	work	In	heat

A knight (chess man), in moving from square to square over the board, converts these disjointed syllables into a verse of poetry. What is the verse?

No. 451.—Proverbial "Pi."

A a c e e e f f h h i i i i i m n n o o o p r r s s t t t. Out of these letters form a truthful proverb.

No. 452.—Reversible Words.

(a) Read forward, I am to wind; read backward, I am to look obliquely. (b) Read forward, I am the face of a timepiece; read backward, I am set down. (c) Read forward, I am a number; read backward, I am a snare. (d) Read forward, I am a resinous substance; read backward, I am a small animal.

No. 453.—Quibbles.

(a) How must I draw a circle around a person placed in the centre of a room so that he will not be able to jump out of it though his legs should be free?

(b) If five times four are thirty-three, what will the fourth of twenty be?

(c) What is the difference between twice twenty-five and twice five and twenty?

Robert Merry printed several such books from *Merry's Museum*. Here are two of his letter rebuses:

Add two strokes to IIII and make nothing

What is this word - 10050055N?

Puzzle constructors began to adopt noms-de-plume around 1870. Unlike the anonymous puzzlers of the past who were embarrassed to admit their fondness for puzzles, this new generation of pen-name puzzlers served to create an aura of mysticism around the art of puzzling. How much more intriguing to solve a puzzle composed by Aldebaran than to solve one penned by John Doe!

The publications devoted exclusively to puzzles were small, short-lived ventures, but they spurred a tremendous fraternal spirit among their subscribers. The first strictly puzzle paper came from Auburn, Maine, in January 1875 and lasted approximately twenty months. Specialized puzzle publications, devoted to a single type of puzzle such as the cryptogram or form, also began to appear toward the end of the century and developed their own adherents. So, too, did puzzle leagues. The Eastern Puzzlers' League, forerunner of the National Puzzlers' League, was founded on July 4, 1883, to "promote sociability" among puzzlers and to "raise the standard of the work." These, however, will be discussed in greater detail in the chapter on "Puzzle Leagues."

Thus the aggregate became more than the sum of its parts. Puzzling developed a mystique of its own as a fraternal spirit blossomed among constructors and solvers alike and puzzling was brought within reach of every literate adult and child. No longer would puzzles be considered ephemera tied to a particular magazine. No longer were they too literate for the "average" person. In changing from an artistic expression of the most educated people of the times to a witty manifestation capable of being posed or solved by any creative mind, puzzling secured a stronghold in the hobby arena which it has maintained to the present time. Puzzling was definitely here to stay!

A PANOPLY OF PUZZLES PAST

As puzzles evolved, puzzling became a favorite pastime that knew no class bounds. People from different levels of society might not have solved the same type of puzzles, but they did share several things in common: a love of words, a desire to be challenged and a willingness to stimulate their gray matter.

Puzzlers are primarily participators rather than spectators. Like Pavlov's dog, their creative juices immediately start to flow at the sight of a new puzzle. Today's puzzle addict has only to view a blank crossword to instinctively reach for a pencil.

Crosswords, however, were not invented until the second decade of this century. As puzzles were becoming firmly embedded in the culture, people spent their time solving acrostics, anagrams, charades, beheadments, logogriphs, rebuses and so on. Since most of these types no longer appear in the popular presses, this chapter is provided for modern puzzlers.

Acrostics

The acrostic is composed so that the first letter of each line of verse or each answer to a given clue, when read together vertically, forms the answer to the puzzle. In a double acrostic, the last letters also form words or names. Queen Victoria was an avid constructor of acrostics and some puzzle historians believe it was her influence that popularized the form in the mid-nineteenth century. Here is the result of one of her efforts. The initial letters in the answer column spell out the name of an English town, while the final letters, reading upwards, tell what the town is famous for.

A city in Italy	N	aple	S
A river in Germany	E	lb	E
A town in the United States	W	ashingto	N
A town in North America	C	incinnat	I
A town in Holland	A	msterda	M
The Turkish name of Constantinople	S	tambou	L
A town in Bothnia	T	orne	A
A city in Greece	L	epant	O
A circle on the globe	E	clipti	C

This was not a particularly well-constructed puzzle for the definitions were too general. A multitude of responses, all equally valid, were possible and, to be honest, as puzzles go, it's rather dull.

Here is a slightly better and more typical example, a double acrostic found in *Fun,* a weekly London humor magazine, which was inspired by a well-known tragedy of the times. The first part of the verse describes the overall theme; then each subsequent stanza defines one word.

Came evil news across the sea,
  Of homes consumed and lives destroyed.
They call for help, and gladly we
  Decree the means to be employed.
To guard from sickness, want, and cold,
  Those whom, though distant, dear we hold.

1. A word best-fitted to describe
  The worship and the ways
Of that same "light and sweetness" tribe
  Sprung-up of modern days.
To which we owe the germ
  Of this affected term.   1. C ul T

2. Oh, happy schooltimes, youth's bright day
With equal shares of work and play,
  (All toil is manhood's lot).
And happy schoolboys too, than men
  Far happier—in especial, when
  This from their friends they got!   2. H ampe R

3. I never see the Masons deckt
  With aprons, sashes, swords;
But I November's Fifth suspect
  Their fashion-plate affords.   3. I nsigni A

4. A verb that is by gamblers used
  Wherein the dicers stand accused.   4. C o G

5. If you a civilian, temp EDWARD THE THIRD,
  Had told that he uttered a fib,
He'd have whipt out a sharp-pointed blade,
    like a bird,
And have tickled you under the rib.   5. A nelac E

6. 'Tis for an implement
  That I am simply meant,
Of my use any miner,
  Will prove a definer.   6. G a D

7. On outspread wing long hovered he,
  Then plunging down into the sea,—
Down-down beneath the wave's white spray
  He dived and caught his finny prey.   7. O spre Y

46

This puzzle was overly long and the verse was somewhat cumbersome. However, it was an extremely ambitious undertaking on the constructor's part. By drawing attention to the Chicago Fire in this unusual manner, it graphically points out that puzzles are a product of their time and, as such, reflect the social, literary or historical milieu in which they were constructed.

The following puzzle with a double acrostic solution is from a children's magazine, *Our Young Folks,* published in 1862. The "foundation words" give the theme of the double acrostic solution, and each of the lines under "cross-words" defines one of the basic horizontal elements from which the double acrostic will emerge.

Foundation Words

Faithful and brave was the band we bore
To seek a home on a stranger's shore.

Cross-words

The swiftest of coursers cannot rival my speed,	S	tea	M
Come to me, if of friends you think you're in need,	P	hiladelphi	A
I am sometimes a passion of hideous mien.	E	nv	Y
Again as a fairy I dance on the green.	E	I	F
My servants love darkness far better than light.	D	evi	L
The scene I have been of a terrible fight.	W	aterlo	O
The manner in which to treat evil we're told.	E	sche	W
A river much sung of by poets of old.	L	eth	E
Without me you ne'er can earn honor or gold.	L	abo	R

Some acrostics were written not as puzzles but as tributes to a loved one. The first letter of each line would spell out the intended name. This acrostic to Gertrude is one example taken from a whole series published in *Dick's Original Album-Verses and Acrostics* in 1879. With this book, and pen and paper, any man could impress his loved one with an "original" name poem. This one was for Gertrude:

Graceful and winning, frank and free
Each movement marked with modesty;
Rosy thy path; thy manner shows
The consciousness of self-repose.
Rest thee, O lady, calm and still,
Under no fear of coming ill.
Deem it not flattery when I say
Envy and hate avoid thy way.

Anagrams

As we have already seen in "Puzzle Origins," anagrams were known to the ancient Greeks and Romans, but they didn't

"My Kingdom for an anagram." Had Henry IV been more of a puzzler, he might have avoided the ruinous result of Ravillac's rage. Perhaps it was Henry's disastrous example that prompted Louis XIII, his son and successor, to hire a Royal Anagrammatist.

really become popular until they were adopted by the Jewish Cabalists in the thirteenth century, at which point they spread rapidly to the learned populace of many nations. People enjoyed rearranging letters to discover unusual relationships between a name and its possible anagrams.

Not every king was as lucky as Louis XIII, who was able to employ his own royal anagrammatist, but some, like Charles IX of France, had courtiers who could compose flattering anagrams of their girlfriend's name. MARIE TOUCHET anagrammatized to JE CHARME TOUT (I charm everyone) was a delightful way to compliment a loved one—remember that I and J were interchangeable in those days.

Overzealous anagrammatists were sometimes foiled by their own weapon. Eleanor Davies, the wife of the poet Sir John

48

Davies, was brought to court because of her prophecies against Charles I. In her defense, she stated that she thought the spirit of Daniel was in her because her name could be anagrammatized into REVEAL O DANIEL. The court attempted to dispossess the spirit from her by anagrammatizing DAME ELEANOR DAVIES into NEVER SO MAD A LADIE. The laughter of the audience so dispirited her that she never prophesied again. Actually these were both imperfect anagrams because not all the letters were used, but it does show how seriously anagramming was viewed.

When anagrams were used to justify an event after its occurrence, the results could be startling. Shortly after Henry IV of France was assassinated in 1610 by a man named Ravillac, it was discovered, to everyone's astonishment, that HENRICUS IV GALLIARUM REX (the Latinized version of Henry IV, King of the Franks), when rearranged, became IN HERUM EXURGIS RAVILLAC (From these Ravillac rises up). Undoubtedly Henry would have preferred this revelation to have been made before his untimely death!

Political upsets could also spark anagrammatists into action. After Disraeli defeated Gladstone in Parliament, two equally appropriate anagrams were bandied about. GLADSTONE was rearranged into G. LEADS NOT and DISRAELI into I LEAD SIR.

As originally constructed, anagrams were rearrangements of names into words without any similarity of meaning. Thus, as we have seen already, AROUET, L.J. transposed his given name into VOLTAIRE, the famous nom-de-plume. As anagrams expanded to include words, phrases and sayings as appropriate starting-off points, the construction requirements remained the same: juggle the original letters to form a new word or phrase. In this manner many mundane anagrams appeared in numerous publications. MACHINE became NICE HAM, CONGRATULATE was rearranged to ON REAL CATGUT, and so forth.

Some puzzle constructors, however, saw how much more exciting anagramming became if the transposed letters were somehow related to the original word(s). The accolades given to such anagrams as PRESBYTERIAN — BEST IN PRAYER, TELEGRAPH — GREAT HELP and REVOLUTION — TO LOVE RUIN, ultimately led to a revision in the rules of anagram construction. As Majolica of the National Puzzlers' League defined it, the perfect anagram "demands that the new word or phrase evolved shall be equivalent in meaning to that whence it was derived. Obviously, this is a severe requirement; and a perfect anagram is, in consequence, a *chef d'oeuvre* of the puzzleistic art." Although this limitation narrowed the field for anagram constructors, it is interesting to note that many anagrams handed down from the past had more or less met this requirement.

49

a) GAVE US A DAMNED CLEVER SATIRE

c) GOVERN, CLEVER LAD

b) GREATEST BORN IDEALIST

d) THE DOOR RING TIDED ILL

For perspicacious puzzlers only—a positively provocative portrait gallery to test your anagrammatic acumen. (*See* Picture Answers, 5.)

The following anagrams appeared in specialized puzzle papers in the late 1800s. All have multiple-word answers, some of which are proper nouns, and each phrase is directly related to its answer:

WHAT ROILS MEN	MOTHERS-IN-LAW
CAN RUIN A SELECTED VICTIM	CIRCUMSTANTIAL EVIDENCE
SLIGHT-FED MEN HAILING PORT	THE LANDING OF THE PILGRIMS
SIGN LONG WEDDED	GOLDEN WEDDINGS

Although anagrams were predominantly presented in the same manner as those above, an occasional constructor would embellish his creation with a witty verse. The following is a clever poem about Saint Valentine's Day, which contained a fitting anagram of the holiday in its final line.

> **Can it be, as legends say,**
> **That this fête of friendly mirth—**
> **Cupid's gayest gala-day—**
> **In a saintly brain had birth?**
> **A quaint**
> **Old saint**
> **He was, I guess,**
> **Who could**
> **Have wooed**
> **His sweet saintess**
> **With such soft vanities as these,**
> **Of tinsel, lace and fripperies!**
> **Could a stern and monkish mind**
> **E'er have such a work designed—**
> **Such an airy, fairy bit?**
> **NAY, A LASS INVENTED IT.**

When it was discovered that definitions, opposite in meaning, could also be derived from words or phrases, the antigram was born. This transposition of CROCODILE into DOCILE ORC and DIPLOMACY to MAD POLICY stimulated puzzlers to compose antigrams such as these:

ARGUE? NAH!	**HARANGUE**
HAPPIEST	**EPITAPHS**
DEMON ALE	**LEMONADE**
UNTIED	**UNITED**

Charades

Charades were entirely unknown to the ancients and their exact origin is disputed by puzzle historians. Isaac D'Israeli, author of *Curiosities of Literature* (1856), states that "The charade is of recent birth, and I cannot discover the origin of this species of logographs. It was not known in France so late as in 1771." The word *charade* is generally believed to be a derivative of the Italian *schiarare* meaning "to disentangle or to clear up." In this type of puzzle a word is broken down into its component syllables, each of which must be guessed before combining the parts into a whole. Charades may be written in verse or prose and the syllables are referred to as "my first," "my second," etc.

Forerunners of charades appeared in the *London Magazine*

in the 1750s and were based on the names of people or places, such as this one about an English town:

To places where ships are safe from a storm
Add that which makes part of your face;
And when these two are together, they'll form
The name of a very brave place.

Portsmouth

Charades were first introduced in the late eighteenth century and soon became one of the most popular puzzle types. They carved out a niche for themselves fairly rapidly and were even mentioned in the 1797 edition of the *Encyclopedia Britannica*: "The exercise of charades, if not greatly constructive, is at least innocent and amusing. At all events, as it has made its way into every fashionable circle, it will scarcely be deemed unworthy of attention."

During the nineteenth century some very famous literary people turned their talents to puzzling. Winthrop Mackworth Praed, the English author remembered for his humorous verse, authored the following charade which became quite controversial as no one could agree on its answer:

Sir Hilary charged at Agincourt;
Sooth, 'twas an awful day!
And though in that old age of sport
The rufflers of the camp and court
Had little time to pray.
'Tis said Sir Hilary muttered there
Two syllables by way of prayer:
My First to all the brave and proud
Who see to-morrow's sun:
My Next, with her cold and quiet cloud,
To those who find their dewy shroud
Before today's be done:
And both together to all blue eyes
That weep when a warrior nobly dies.

Puzzle historians have reluctantly accepted "good night" as the best answer to this charade.

In the same manner that literature could reflect the writer's philosophical stance, a good puzzle might be more than an amusing diversion. A charade from an 1808 issue of *The Eye*, a weekly literary magazine from Philadelphia, was the vehicle used by an anonymous composer to express his or her views on drinking:

In open view I stand confess'd
Descriptive of a man unbless'd;
And grumble for displeasure;
Two syllables I own, and they

Are both alike, form'd to convey
   My views in even measure.
I've other qualities beside
Those above mention'd, 'tis my pride
   What man to beast will change
Twice to announce; you'll find it plain,
If you will trace me back again,
   And true as it is strange.
Reverse my first and last, and each will tell
What sots desire and love, alas! too well:
My whole for hope and fear admittance find,
And is expressive of a peevish mind.

The answer was expressed in verse in a subsequent issue:

Without the aid of magic touch,
   How often do we see
Man changed to brute by drinking much
   Of RUM or ratafia.
If we reverse the sots delight,
   Then twice the same come o'er—
To MURMUR we will find we write,
   Which all do less or more.
But mostly those who love the RUM,
   Do double the *reverse*;
When they to want and trouble come,
   And fortune proves adverse.

Kitty take those books to the library and get M.rs Brown to change them: tell her I'm fond of the rumantic.

Men were not the only ones guilty of rum-inating in the early 1800s. A subscription to a puzzle-oriented literary magazine might have cured *madame* of her rum-anticism.

Not all charades were as lengthy or as weighty as the previous. To conserve space, short charades like this one were often used in puzzle columns:

> **My first is a sailor,**
> **My second's to gain,**
> **My whole, though oft shot at,**
> **Has never been slain.**

target

The next two charades, from an 1839 book, both had the same answer, though their authors had differing views on the subject:

> **My second is doomed to suffer my first,**
> **But of all that he suffers my whole is the worst.**

> **With a taste of my first my second is curst;**
> **But of all my whole suffers, my second's the worst.**

Woman
The answer to both:

It was charades like these that prompted popular writers such as the Rev. Sydney Smith to term the puzzles "unpardonable trumpery" and recommend that offenders "should instantly be hurried off to execution." Fortunately no one took his advice and nineteenth-century puzzlers were able to produce the following charades:

(a)

My *first* is bashful, my *second* is fastening, and my *whole* is a Shakespearian character.

(b)

My *first* is a vehicle, my *second* is a favorite, and my *whole* is in most drawing rooms.

(c)

> **My *first* gives light and heat;**
> **My *next's* oft used to cheat;**
> **My *whole* it means to cheer**
> **Or "comfort" those most dear.**

(d)

> **My *first* we among the five vowels may see**
> **My *second's* a sweet pretty creature**
> **My *third,* when discovered, will point out to thee**
> **A word of a sorrowful nature.**

alas
solace
carpet
Shylock

Sometimes a charade made use of Roman numerals:

> **Fifty is my *first,* nothing is my *second,***
> **Five just makes my *third.* My *fourth's* a vowel reckoned,**
> **Now to fill my *whole,* put all my parts together;**
> **I die if I get cold, but never fear cold weather.**

love

In this cousin of the charade one chose a single letter from each line of a verse to combine with the others to form a word. Commonly in this type of charade the words in each line were opposites with few, if any, similar letters between them, as in the following example:

First in lamb, but not in sheep,
Second in shallow, not in deep;
Third in rat, but not in mouse;
Fourth in villa, not in house;
Fifth in love, but not in hate;
Sixth in door, but not in gate;
Seventh in plant, but not in tree;
And now a name you plainly see.

Matilda

Conundrums and Riddles

Riddles and conundrums are classified together because the dividing line between them is not very distinct. Both involve propounding questions to receive unexpected answers. Conundrums have been defined as "a play on words in which your wit is exerted to play the fool successfully." Basically they are puns or jokes. One is really not expected to be able to answer them in a true puzzle sense because the relationship between question and answer is so unlikely, as witnessed over the page:

Two details from a color poster (date unknown) parodying the characters from Dickens's *Pickwick Papers*. The artist devised clever conundrums for each of the characters. (*See* Picture Answers, 6 and 7.)

Smangle

5. Of what trade is the sun ?

Bridget Copperphiz

22. Why is a reporter like a forger

How many apples were eaten in the Garden of Eden?
Ten: Eve ate, Adam too.

Why is a good lettuce the most amiable of vegetables?
Because it is all heart.

What is the center of gravity?
The letter v.

In what color should friendship be kept?
In violet.

Why are fatigued persons like a wheel?
Because they are tired.

How many peas in a pint?
One.

In contrast, riddle solving involves a certain amount of reasoning ability as there is some relationship between the riddle and its answer:

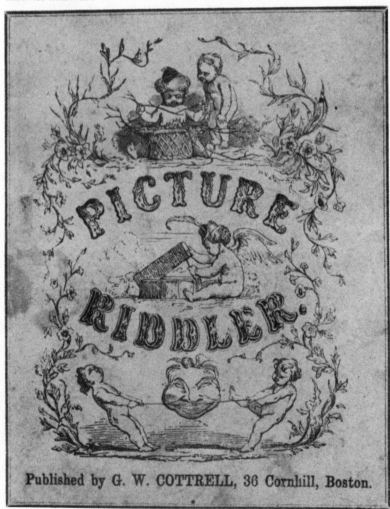

An 1845 book, *Picture Riddler,* had a striking cover to appeal to a wide audience.

Published by G. W. COTTRELL, 36 Cornhill, Boston.

56

A	B	C	D	E	F	G
H	I	J	K	L	M	N
O	P	Q	R	S	T	U
V	W	X	Y	Z	Æ	Œ

96.

IN every gift of Fortune I abound,
In me is every vice and virtue found ;
With black, and blue, and green, myself I paint ;
With me an Atheist stands before a Saint ;
Far above Nature I make Art precede,
And before Sov'reigns give the Poor the lead.
Many who're call'd the learned and the wise,
Did I not help them, you would oft despise.
Nay, more—within my grasp together bound,
The King, the Beggar, and the Clown are found.
In one thing I excel the proudest lords,—
You always may depend upon my words.

Little Riddler.

A E I O U

1.

We are little airy creatures,
All of different voice and features ;
One of us in glass is set ;
One of us you'll find in jet ;
One of us is set in tin ;
And the fourth a box within ;
If the last you should pursue,
It can never fly from you.

What belongs to yourself, yet is used by others more than yourself?

Your name.

What is that which is often brought to table, often cut, but never eaten?

A pack of cards.

What God never sees; what a king seldom sees; what we see every day.

An equal.

Riddles were frequently connected to cataclysmic events in ancient times. In the Oedipus myth the fate of a whole nation was in jeopardy until the crucial riddle was solved. In fairy tales, where a common theme was to pit the brain of the hero against the brawn of the villain, riddle-solving ability was an excellent indicator of mental agility. The *100 Riddles of the Fairy Bellaria,* published in 1892, pits a queen and her puzzle skills against a cruel invading king. Ruggero, the scoundrel king, threatens to destroy the kingdom of Bellaria as well as the good queen's husband unless she can answer all one hundred riddles posed to her. "By thy head, O Queen! answer me this riddle: 'What hast thou often seen fall but never rise?' thundered the king." The good fairy's expertise came through one-hundred fold in answers like "The snow which falls upon the plain, as snow doth never rise again." Ruggero was as poor a sport as Oedipus's Sphinx and was so enraged by the queen's riddling powers that he disintegrated.

Although many riddles of the past were geared to adults, today's riddles are mainly found in children's publications. An ever-popular juvenile verse, "Humpty Dumpty," is actually a riddle. The first two lines of the poem describe Humpty Dump-

Many riddle books used similar themes but exploited them differently. LEFT An enigmatical example of high-quality riddling: a riddle about the alphabet from *Picture Riddler.* RIGHT This page from *Little Riddler* about vowels is not as sophisticated as the alphabet riddle—it was obviously geared to a younger audience.

ty in such a manner that one might think he were a person. It is only when one reaches the part about not being able to mend him that one realizes he's an egg.

Cryptograms

Cryptograms are made by substituting one letter for another throughout a sentence. Easier to construct than solve, the main rule is that no letter may stand for itself.

Many famous people have constructed and solved cryptograms. Lord Bacon was one of the most famous cipher experts. Edgar Allan Poe wrote a story, *The Gold Bug,* in which a cryptogram figured prominently.

Here are a few easy cryptograms. Solvers new to the art are best advised to look for giveaway words such as *a, an, and, the* and *that* to get them started:

(a)

DFC KAIUR KYUU XCMCI WDHIMC TAI KAXRCIW, NJD AXUQ TAI KHXD AT KAXRCI.

(b)

NINP HDN OKFOX YBZZNZ HDN HLEN UT XNNYLPM LHZ DBPCZ URZT.

In more difficult crypts, constructors try to avoid the following: ordinary words; repetition of words; use of the most frequent vowels and consonants; and double letters, especially double vowels and words having the same prefix or suffix. By eliminating as many of these clues as possible, the constructor can devise some challenging crypts:

(a)

MTWYPC LBGU, PZD FGU, LBWMGCZ BH NYBSZUM, HWZMF FGYWEB, CYNZ DBRGP CWZGU ZSGP DFZP RGWLF ZAOYPBK LBRZM PYCF.

(b)

BAD ORGY; TJEGLHAD THROG; BETA CTRBFAH. THUOC CIMROY; IMREG JUDY; FUMGKHN TJEHF. AGY JMDK: TRHEPUM SEVJK.

Ciphers are most useful as a means of transmitting messages through enemy lines during war time. The following message was used in 1862 by Abraham Lincoln during the Civil War:

Burnside, Acquia Creek:
Can Inn Ale me withe 2 oar our Ann pas Ann me flesh ends
N.V. Corn Inn out with U cud Inn heaven day nest Wed Roe
Moore Tom darkey hat Greek Why Hawk of abbott Inn b
chewed I if. — Bates

The world will never starve for wonders, but only for want of wonder.

Even the clock passes the time by keeping its hands busy.

Spring coat, new hat, fresh corsage of violets, give woman great elan when March equinox comes nigh.

Men walk; children crawl; mice scamper. Crows squawk; quail honk; poultry chirp. Elk hunt; caribou fight.

58

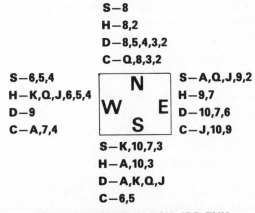

Ciphers were frequently used in war departments to pass messages through enemy lines. This is a facsimile of one telegraphic cipher code from Abraham Lincoln's war office.

This was not a particularly difficult cipher as all one had to do was start reading at the end and continue to the beginning to reveal the following message:

Major-General Burnside, Acquia Creek, Va:

If I should be in boat off Acquia Creek at dark tomorrow (Wednesday) evening, could you, without inconvenience, flesh [meet] me and pass an hour or two with me. A Lincoln

Caliban, a famous British puzzler, composed the following cryptogram. It's unusual in that the code is related to a deck of cards (S, H, C an D stand for Spades, Hearts, Clubs and Diamonds, respectively):

The members of The Enigma Club received early in July the following communication from their secretary:

```
                          S—8
                          H—8,2
                          D—8,5,4,3,2
                          C—Q,8,3,2

   S—6,5,4           ┌─────────┐    S—A,Q,J,9,2
   H—K,Q,J,6,5,4     │    N    │    H—9,7
   D—9               │ W     E │    D—10,7,6
   C—A,7,4           │    S    │    C—J,10,9
                     └─────────┘
                          S—K,10,7,3
                          H—A,10,3
                          D—A,K,Q,J
                          C—6,5

          XVWXRCHOLHPJX YCK JPB ZVK.
```

What was the purpose of this communication?

The fact that the King of Clubs is missing points to this as being the key word of the crypt. The key is obtained by writing out the key word "KING OF CLUBS," followed by the remaining letters of the alphabet (that is, all remaining letters not found in the key word), in two lines of thirteen letters each:

K I N G O F C L U B S A D
E H J M P Q R T V W X Y Z

Then substitute for every letter in the cryptogram the letter above or below it in the key: K equals E, H equals I and so on. Deciphered, the message reads simply: SUBSCRIPTIONS ARE NOW DUE.

Perhaps more books have been written about cryptograms than any other type of puzzle. Today there is even an American Cryptogram Association (see the chapter entitled "Puzzle Leagues" for a greater discussion).

Enigmas

The word *enigma* comes from the Greek verb signifying "to darken and hide," and is a puzzle in which the word to be guessed is alluded to by veiled references. The parables of the Hebrews, the oracles of the Greeks, the fables of Aesop and the proverbs of the Persians were all forms of enigmas.

Jonathan Swift, author of *Gulliver's Travels*, became an enigma composer and solver after being introduced to them by his friends. Here is his enigma about "a fan which a lady holds in her muff":

> From India's burning clime I'm brought,
> With cooling gales like zephyrs fraught.
> Not Iris, when she paints the sky,
> Can show more different hues than I;
> Nor can she change her form so fast,
> I'm now a sail, and now a mast.
> I here am red, and there am green,
> A beggar there and here a queen.
> I sometimes live in house of hair,
> And oft in hand of lady fair.
> I please the young, I grace the old,
> And am at once both hot and cold
> Say what I am then, if you can,
> And find the rhyme, and you're the man.

This excerpt from an enigma on the letter "H", attributed to Lord Byron but actually written by Catherine Fanshawe, shows how cleverly clues could be camouflaged:

'Twas whispered in Heaven, 'twas muttered in Hell,
And Echo caught faintly the sound as it fell.

One of the most famous enigmas of all was composed by George Canning, who served for a short time as Prime Minister of England:

A word there is of plural number,
Foe to ease and tranquil slumber;
Any other word you take
And add an *s* will plural make.
But if you add an *s* to this,
So strange the metamorphosis;
Plural is plural now no more,
And sweet what bitter was before.

cares—caress

Enigmatic questions were very popular in ancient times at games and feasts. The Renaissance was also a fruitful period for enigmas, and as puzzling became popular with mass audiences enigmas were the puzzles most often found in books and magazines. Although some prose enigmas do exist, many of the best ones were composed in verse:

My two first letters are a man, my three first a woman,
My four first a brave man, my whole a brave woman.

he-her-hero-heroine

The beginning of eternity;
The end of time and space;
The beginning of every end,
And the end of every place.

the letter "E"

I'm tall and square made; by my neighbors most seen;
Am partly without doors, and partly within;
I always stand still, and ne'er go to bed
The food I take in goes out at my head.
If my stomach's o'ercharged, assistance is found,
Which cures, but ne'er fails to proclaim it around.
Of late I have been more than usual opprest
With a kind of whirligig placed in my breast.
I'm often so hot, that there are many days,
When a spark, I may say, would set me in blaze.

chimney

Hidden or Buried Words

Hidden words were not too taxing on the brain. They were merely sentences so composed that they contained, without transposition, buried words:

YOU CAN CROSS THE BRIDGE OR GET A BOAT.

61

It takes a while to accustom your eye, but if you study the example, GEORGE should pop out at you in the second half of the sentence.

Hidden word games were used for parties and were frequent alternatives to book teas. In fact, books of buried words were written with perforated edges so that the pages could be pulled out and each guest given a sheet. The emphasis then was on speed; the first one to correctly identify all the buried words would receive a prize. Can you find the names hidden in the following sentences?

Ada **YOU CAN GO BY STEAMER TO CANADA.**

William or Seth **WILL I AMUSE THE REMAINING GUESTS?**

Amelia **THE WHITE CAMEL I ADMIRE MOST.**

Susan **HE PROMISES US A NICE BOTTLE OF WINE.**

Esther **A BRAVE MAN DEFIES THE ROBBER.**

Grace **THE INTERESTING RACES COME OFF LAST.**

Emma **HE SAW THEM MADE AT THE PALACE.**

Logographs

Logographs cover a wide variety of puzzles such as beheadments, curtailments, syncopations, transpositions and reversals, all of which involve letter manipulation. In a beheadment the first letter of a word is removed to form a new word; in a curtailment the same thing is done to the last letter; in a syncopation any letter can be removed. A transposition consists of two entirely different words using the same letters, and in a reversal two words can be turned into each other by reading them backwards.

It was puzzles such as these that were responsible for the evolution of puzzles from literary expressions to amusing pastimes. Rarely were these puzzles couched in the sort of esoteric verse that had characterized enigmas and charades. Rather, constructors wrote in short, witty rhymes or even prose. The following examples are typical of the entertaining and manipulative-type puzzles that appeared in mass-marketed magazines such as *The Masquerade* in England and *The Saturday Evening Post* in the United States:

skill **Take away one letter, and I murder; take away two and I am dying, if the whole does not save me.**

wheel-heel-eel

> **My whole is a circle complete;**
> **Beheaded I'm part of the feet;**
> **Behead me again if you wish,**
> **'Twill bring to your notice a fish.**

SHAKSPEARIAN

PLAYS.

TRIO.

FOLSOM

Puzzles sometimes appeared in magazines as filler items, such as this one from *Demorest's Monthly Magazine,* late nineteenth century, which required readers to find the names of three Shakespearian plays which were camouflaged in a circle of letters. (*See* Picture Answers, 8.)

Three of Shakspeare's plays are concealed in this circle of letters. Select a letter to start with, and then take every third letter. For instance: start at T No. 5, K No. 8 would be the next letter to use, then B 11, and so on. This succession of letters does not make any word as you will observe, but it serves to show the plan of working the puzzle. By patient searching you will find the titles of three well known plays from Shakspeare.

My total is a brilliant gem,
I deck the costly diadem;
Erase a letter, and I stand
High honour'd in the royal land;
Cut off the last, my first regain,
A well-known fruit I do explain.

pearl-earl-pear

Syncopate a Spanish horse,
  One that is small in size,
And by the change a man appears,
  To everyone's surprise.

genet-gent

Part of a foot with good judgment transpose,
And the answer you'll find just under your nose.

inch-chin

There are two words, three letters each,
  Which show to you the name
Of what is used too frequently,
  And likely to inflame.
Reverse these, then, and oft you'll find
  Resulting from this cause
A frequent crime, about the worst
  That's mentioned in our laws.

red rum-rum-murder

"The Little Brown Jug," composed for a temperance union by the great puzzle constructor Sam Loyd. The object of the puzzle is to count the number of times the palindrome RED RUM & MURDER could be read in the little brown jug. (*See* Picture Answers, 9.)

The answer to the last puzzle is a topic that has been popular with many puzzle constructors, as we have already seen in the charade on page 53. Sam Loyd, one of the first people to derive a lot of money from puzzles, also used this topic as the theme for a puzzle he constructed for a temperance organization (see left).

Palindromes

Also known as reciprocal verses, palindromes are words or phrases which read the same backwards and forwards. Tot, toot, peep, solos, redder, level, civic, madam and tenet are examples of palindromic words; while Otto, Hannah, Anna and Bob have names which they can easily spell backwards or forwards. YREKA BAKERY is an establishment selling pastries; RED RUM DID EMIT REVEL ERE LEVER TIME DID MURDER might be a teetotaler's warning (again this recurring theme pops up!); while rodent headliners might be billed as STAR RATS. Because of the inherent difficulty in getting sentences to read the same both backwards and forwards, palindromes by nature are more fun than profound, as these specimens show:

What to say when the kitchen help wants to quit
STOP O POTS

Why non-coms don't like pining gals
SIGHS ABASH G.I.S.

Coed's hotline message about Herb
PASS UP "MACABRE HERB" A CAMPUS SAP

What to say when a feline rushes past
WAS IT A CAT I SAW?

Teacher's goals
DRAW PUPILS LIP UPWARD

Rebuses

A rebus is a hieroglyphic riddle formed either pictorially or literally. In the latter case, letters, figures, Roman numerals or punctuation marks are used to represent words or phrases. A clever example of a literal rebus is shown in the following correspondence:

A gentleman who had sent to a certain city for a carload of fuel, wrote this to his nephew residing there:

> **Dear Nephew**
>
> ;
>
> **Uncle John**

Presently he received the following reply:

> **Dear Uncle**
>
> :
>
> **James**

In an extremely brief manner the uncle had asked the nephew to "See my coal on" (semicolon), while the nephew replied "Coal on" (colon).

Here are other samples of rebuses involving literal interpretation:

KIN⌐ = a celebrated line from Shakespeare

OF-OF-OF-OF-OF-OF-OF-OF-OF-OF = a common word

To three-fourths of a cross, add a circle complete;
Then let two semi-circles a perpendicular meet;
Next, add a triangle that stands on two feet;
Then, two semi-circles, and a circle complete.

Rebuses involving the use of Roman numerals were also popular:

Another ingenious rebus—a French optician's sign said to be designed by the artist James Mc-Neill Whistler. The sign reads, of course, "*Au petit chien*" (the little dog) - a close phonetic equivalent to OPTICIEN.

"A little more than kin and less than kind."

oftentimes

tobacco

Game manufacturers took advantage of the public's fascination with "picture puzzles" to develop this rebus card game. The rules were flexible: the game could be played as solitaire or in groups, the object being to decipher as many rebus cards as possible. Categories were varied and included countries, famous people and proverbs. (*See* Picture Answers, 10.)

A PROVERB

A PROVERB

Rebuses traditionally were a combination of pictures and words. The pictures did not necessarily have to be related to the story, but they did have to be phonetically accurate enough to suggest the pronunciation of the word or syllables they represented. This rebus is a well-known nursery rhyme. (*See* Picture Answers, 11.)

Milan

1000 + NAIL = an Italian town

leopard

550 + OPERA = an animal

Five hundred, a thousand and one,
With proper attention dispose;
And that kind of light will appear

dim

Which the sun in a fog often shows.

66

Some of the most unusual rebuses involve positioning words so that a graphic shorthand evolves. EIGHT COME NINE is an example of a witty and brief dinner invitation asking guests to "come" between "eight" and "nine" o'clock. The next few rebuses all involve unusual placement of words:

(a)

I am

man making mischief wife

I am above making mischief between man and wife.

(b)

size

Antoinette

age

Antoinette is under-size but is not underage.

(c)

the fate of a belle: xxEE marriage XXee

Small crosses and great ease before marriage; large crosses and little ease after marriage.

(d)

and

standing   towering   man judges man

The   mind

The understanding and overtowering mind judges between man and man.

(e)

There is an   vice difference virtue

whelming

There is an over-whelming difference between vice and virtue.

PICTORIAL PROVERBS.

A wise son maketh a glad father, but a foolish son is the heaviness of his mother.

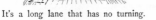

It's a long lane that has no turning.

15

HIEROGLYPHIC PROVERB.

He that walketh with wise men shall be wise, but the companion of fools shall be destroyed.

14

Pictorial proverbs from a nineteenth-century puzzle book called *Guess Me* (undated).

Sometimes rebus makers were a little too clever, as this anecdote indicates:

A naughty boy once sent the following letter to his schoolmaster:
2 X u r, 2 X u b,
I c u r 2 X for me.

The schoolmaster made this reply:
2 yy u r, 2 yy u b,
I c u r 2 yy for me.

And very properly gave him a whipping in the bargain!

Creative rebus making was rewarding for an itinerant beggar. In an area where pandhandling was illegal, an enterprising chap hung the following sign around his neck:

He so aroused the curiosity of the numerous passers-by that they were willing to "buy" the answer to his rebus. He had turned puzzle making into a profitable business without breaking the law.

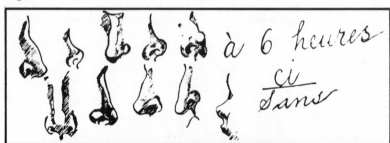

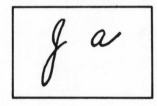

The next few rebuses show the diversity of this form of puzzling:

(a)

Express the following in words, the first in English and the second in French.

1. AL
    |
    L

2. TOU
    |
    T

Too cross you are, too cross you be, I see you are too cross for me.

Too wise you are, too wise you be, I see you are too wise for me.

For a long period I ate next to nothing.

A dinner invitation received by the writer Du Maurier, in the form of a literal rebus using words and symbols. *"Diner a six heures sans souci"* (Dinner at 6 o'clock without care) was the message: *Dix nez* (ten noses) *à 6 heures ci/sans* – *"sans" sou* (under) *"ci."*

Du Maurier's acceptance was exquisitely simple. It employed a large "J" (*"J" grand*) and a small "a" (*"a" petit*) to answer *J'ai grand appetit* (I have a big appetite).

1. All hath an ending here below.
2. Tout est fini ici bas.

68

(b)

A teacher placed the following message on the board to reduce tattling in the classroom:

> Doun Toot Her Sasy
> Ouw Ould Bed on
> Eby.

(c)

Workmen thought they had unearthed a rare archaeological find when they came upon a stone with the following inscription. Did they?

```
              BENE
    AT.  HTH  .IS  ST
    ONERE  .POS  .ET
H.  CLAUD.  COS.  TERT
            R.I.P.
      ES.  ELLE.  RO
          F.  IMP
IN G.  TONAS  .DO
     TH  . HISCO
        N SORT J
        A.N.E.
```

Do unto others as you would be done by.

They didn't. The words read as follows: Beneath this stone reposeth Claud Coster, tripe seller of Impington, as doth his consort Jane.

Unsecret message

A countryside instruction. The farmer wasn't a foreigner or a secret agent. What was he saying?

Sometimes a "coded" puzzle merely requires one's ability to read something a little differently. (*See* Picture Answers, 12.)

Word Squares and Other Forms

Word squares and other geometric shapes utilize diagrams in their construction and are thus called form puzzles. When some of the first word squares were introduced in *Godey's Lady's Book and Magazine* in 1862, there was no indication of how popular form puzzles would ultimately become: almost all twentieth-century puzzling involves the use of forms.

When word squares first began to attract attention, the most common sizes were 4 x 4, 5 x 5 and 6 x 6. Here are two examples from the early 1870s:

```
S E D A T E          W A S H E S

E L E V E N          A R T E R Y

D E F E A T          S T O R M S

A V E R S E          H E R M I T

T E A S E R          E R M I N E

E N T E R S          S Y S T E M
```

Clues were generally the same type as those presented in today's crosswords. Occasionally verse was used:

My first is to exist,	L I V E
My second is the same;	I B I D
My third is something bad;	V I L E
My fourth a garden's name.	E D E N

As puzzlers became more adept at composing word squares the size of the squares increased. However, to form a 9 x 9 square obscure words which were not generally in one's everyday vocabulary had to be included:

```
Q U A R E L E S T

U P P E R E S T E

A P P O I N T E R

R E O M E T E R S

E R I E V I L L E

L E N T I L L I N

E S T E L L I N E

S T E R L I N G S

T E R S E N E S S
```

Puzzles such as the above were too esoteric for a mass audience and even turned off some regular enthusiasts. One puzzler complained, "Must one abandon all business effort and social pastime to labor in libraries in search for references? Is this fair? Is this how Puzzledom is to be preserved?"

Fortunately for the hordes of puzzle fans who welcome a challenge but are repelled by such reliance on obscure terminology, these puzzles died a natural death. Today, they are generally found only in specialized puzzle publications whose intrepid subscribers zealously attack and conquer difficult word squares.

To provide diversity other form puzzles were devised. Diamonds, rhomboids, pyramids, octagons and half-squares were found in publications during the last quarter of the nineteenth century and had a steady following until the crossword took over as the world's most popular form puzzle. Examples of these unusual form puzzles show how visually exciting and diverse these puzzles were. In most of the forms, the same words read across and down; the rhomboid and pyramid, however, have different words for the *across* and *down* columns:

DIAMOND
```
      H
    F O R
  F I N I S
H O N E S T Y
  R I S K Y
    S T Y
      Y
```

RHOMBOID
```
T R A C K
A R E N A
  E D E N S
  E A T E R
    D E T E R
```

OCTAGON
```
    P A D
    P O R E S
  P A L A T E S
P O L Y G O N A L
A R A G O N I T E
D E T O N A T E D
  S E N I T E S
  S A T E S
    L E D
```

PYRAMID
```
L O C O M O T I V E S
  S A T I R I C A L
    M I N A R E T
      C O T E S
        R O D
          R
```

HALF-SQUARE
```
E A S T E R N
A L P I N E
S P U R S
T I R E
E N S
R E
N
```

Although these puzzles were entertaining and challenging, they virtually disappeared from popular magazines and newspapers when the crossword invaded puzzledom. Today many of them exist only in puzzle league magazines which cater to hardcore puzzle addicts.

CROSSWORD CRAZE

The blank crossword, uncluttered and perfectly symmetrical challenges the solver to conquer it. Millions of people throughout the world get an itchy feeling at the mere sight of a blank crossword. No day of theirs is complete without a bout of crossword solving. They'll purchase the newspaper or magazine that carries their favorite brand of crossword and will religiously attack the puzzle day after day usually at the same time every day. The sense of accomplishment that they get from solving a puzzle lasts only until the next blank puzzle crosses their horizon and the whole solving mechanism begins anew.

The crossword started out as a space filler in a corner of a newspaper column, took the world by surprise in the 1920s and today is found in practically every newspaper published. Politicians, royalty and movie stars—along with us more ordinary mortals, of course—are avid enthusiasts and there's no sign of obsolescence more than sixty years after its birth.

Why? What lures so many faithful followers to those black and white squares? The motivations are as varied as the puzzlists themselves, but all crossword addicts agree that they wouldn't want to go through life without their opiate.

The crossword was introduced to the public inauspiciously on December 21, 1913. Arthur Wynne, editor of the "Fun" page for *The New York World* constructed a "word cross" as a filler. The puzzle was an extension of the word diamond, the major variation being that the vertical words were not the same as the horizontal words. Readers reacted almost immediately to the new puzzle and inundated Wynne with their own constructions. Gradually the original design was altered to the now familiar square shape with patterned black and white boxes. The puzzle attracted a limited but devoted following and the newspaper received complaints if the puzzle was missing or if it contained too many typographical errors. (The typesetters at *The World* were less enthusiastic than most people about the new puzzle for it meant more work for them. Consequently, some of the early puzzles were riddled with errors and were extremely difficult to solve.)

In 1920, partly to appease complaining readers, the editors

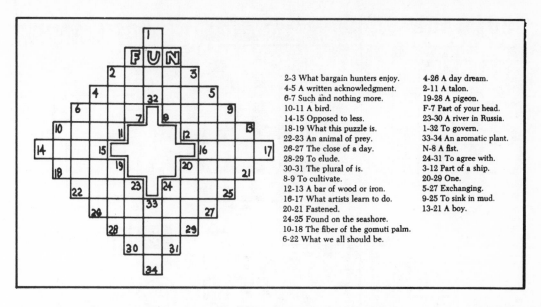

FUN

2-3 What bargain hunters enjoy.
4-5 A written acknowledgment.
6-7 Such and nothing more.
10-11 A bird.
14-15 Opposed to less.
18-19 What this puzzle is.
22-23 An animal of prey.
26-27 The close of a day.
28-29 To elude.
30-31 The plural of is.
8-9 To cultivate.
12-13 A bar of wood or iron.
16-17 What artists learn to do.
20-21 Fastened.
24-25 Found on the seashore.
10-18 The fiber of the gomuti palm.
6-22 What we all should be.

4-26 A day dream.
2-11 A talon.
19-28 A pigeon.
F-7 Part of your head.
23-30 A river in Russia.
1-32 To govern.
33-34 An aromatic plant.
N-8 A fist.
24-31 To agree with.
3-12 Part of a ship.
20-29 One.
5-27 Exchanging.
9-25 To sink in mud.
13-21 A boy.

assigned the crossword puzzle to a new secretary, Margaret Petherbridge (later Farrar). She did her job so well that she became the unofficial crossword editor. Gradually the quality of the puzzles was raised. Mistakes were minimized, definitions were limited to dictionary words, and unclued letters were eliminated. Rules for constructors were mailed out to contributors and the puzzles generally became more uniform.

Like other puzzles that have come and gone, the crossword might have languished and died a natural death had it not been for Simon and Schuster's foray into the publishing world in 1924. They were eager to publish their first book and were open to suggestions for a suitable title. Mr. Simon's aunt remarked that a friend of hers would love a book of crossword puzzles similar to those in *The World* but that there didn't seem to be any available. Thinking that such a book had sales potential, Simon and Schuster approached the editors of *The World*—Margaret Petherbridge, Prosper Buranelli and F. Gregory Hartswick—and offered them a seventy-five dollar advance to compile fifty puzzles for such a book. Drawing on their supply of unused puzzles, the editors compiled the book within three months. In the interim, Simon and Schuster had been getting some negative reactions about the intended project and had second thoughts about putting their names on it (after all, they were Harvard fellows!). Instead, they decided to crib the name of their telephone exchange and publish it under the imprint of The Plaza Publishing Company. The rest is history. The world literally went berserk over this first crossword book. Although the initial printing had been for a cautious 3,600 copies, by the end of the year, through reprints and new series, a total of 350,000 crossword books had been sold.

Arthur Wynne's first "word cross" creation as it appeared in *The New York World* in 1913. No one was more surprised at the crossword's rise to popularity than Mr. Wynne. He left *The World* before the first crossword book was published and maintained a low profile throughout the craze. (*See* Picture Answers, 13.)

BULMACA

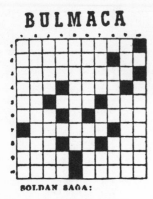

BOLDAN SAGA:

ONNEPI KÖNYVHÉT

Concurso de crucigramas

TIDSFORDRIV

TEKA TEKL SILANG

Σταυρόλεξον

ΣΤΑΥΡΟΛΕΞΟΝ ΥΠ' ΑΡΙΘ. 1843

MOTS CROISÉS

PROBLEME Nº 259

ONS BLOKKIES RAAISEL NO. 12

КРОССВОРД

The crossword spread rapidly throughout the world and each country adopted its own format.

Crosswords showed up at the most unlikely places. The University of Kentucky put them in their college curriculum. A Princeton professor offered a prize for a puzzle having two different correct solutions. Hoping to increase church attendance, a minister in Pittsburgh printed crossword puzzles on a blackboard and invited the congregation to puzzle out the text before the sermon began. The Baltimore and Ohio Railroad put dictionaries on all its main-line trains to accommodate passengers who armed themselves with puzzle books to occupy them during their journeys.

Ads for crossword puzzle parties appeared in magazines and newspapers. Packs made up of several copies of the same puzzle printed on stiff cardboard were offered for sale, making it possible for several people to work concurrently on the same puzzle. Parties became combat arenas where guests would be expected to compete with each other for the fastest solution to the puzzle. Crossword matches were held at public places such as Wanamaker's Auditorium in New York, where frenzied crowds would cheer on competing college students.

The epidemic wasn't confined to the United States. Like the flu and just as contagious, the bug crossed the ocean and attacked England and the Continent. They too succumbed to the craze. The English royal family was rumored to have tried it and liked it! Dublin newspapers offered a £5,000 first prize in a crossword contest. Dutch firms used the puzzle as a gimmick in advertising campaigns, while the Viennese became adept at solving crosswords while imbibing coffee and whipped cream.

Dictionary and thesaurus sales increased dramatically. As a gimmick, pencils were attached to crossword books. Pocket dictionaries became fashionable, and crossword jewelry was offered for sale.

Puzzles even invaded show business and vaudeville. An Elsie Janis Broadway revue entitled *Puzzles of 1925* satirized the fad in a scene depicting a sanitorium for crossword puzzle fans dur-

LEFT To cash in on the craze, jewelry designers offered these unusual crossword bracelets, rings and collar pins.

RIGHT Since crosswords could be done anywhere, it was important to be prepared for the next bout of solving by having the appropriate reference books immediately at hand!

CROSS WORD PUZZLE SANITORIUM

There was lavish praise for this crossword scene from Elsie Janis's Broadway revue, *Puzzles of 1925*, from both the critics and the public. Perhaps its appeal lay in the fact that the satirization hit a nerve with the audience.

ing which an attending physician tried to "cure" his patients who had gone mad trying to solve crossword puzzles. This scenario wasn't as exaggerated as it appeared. Some events in real life nearly paralleled those on the stage.

Not everyone, however, was so enthusiastic about the puzzle. One woman, calling herself a crossword widow, sued her husband for support. The judge, while denying her request, did limit the husband to three puzzles a day so that he could maintain his job and provide for his family.

In another instance, three diners at a restaurant were so involved with solving a difficult puzzle that they ignored the proprietor's requests to leave the establishment at closing time. Frustrated by their refusal, the owner called the police. When arrests were made and the puzzle devotees sentenced to ten days in jail, all the parties involved were satisfied with the verdict: the proprietor had his revenge and the puzzlists were overjoyed at the prospect of having so much time to do their puzzle in a quiet four-letter place!

Producers of mah-jongg sets felt the greatest impact of the crossword craze, for their sales were drastically reduced when the world turned its attention to puzzles. Cartoons appeared in the popular magazines labeling those still playing mah-jongg as

"Old-fashioned! Why, my dear, she still plays mah-jongg"

Mah-jongg had been an extremely popular game prior to the crossword's appearance. When the world became obsessed with the crossword, sales of mah-jongg sets plummeted. Cartoons such as this one didn't boost sales either.

This Picture Has No Title

$1,000.00 in Prizes to the Winners of this Title Contest. See following Conditions:

For the best titles to this cartoon, LIFE will award prizes as follows:

FIRST PRIZE.................. $500   THIRD PRIZE................ $150
SECOND PRIZE............... $300   FOURTH PRIZE.............. $50

Life magazine's "Name a Crossword Scene" contest ran for two months. The first prize offer was $500, quite a tidy sum in 1924. Of the 138,250 responses, the judges picked "The game that separated Pa from Ma Jong" as the best title.

being behind the times. Perhaps the line that best sums up the puzzle's impact on mah-jongg is the winning title chosen in late 1924 by *Life* magazine in their "Name a Crossword Scene" contest—"The Game that separated Pa from Ma Jong." The fact that 1,500 entries carried the title of "The Bore" or "The Pest" is indicative of the negative attitude that some people already felt toward the puzzle. The mah-jongg makers were so frustrated and distressed by their loss of sales that they publicly vented their anger at the crossword editors through a Valentine's Day message in *The New Yorker* magazine in 1925:

**Roses are red, violets are blue
We'd like to cut your throats for you.**

No puzzle had ever before obsessed the public like the crossword. Although some of the events prophesied by Neal O'Hara, a popular writer of the time, never materialized—crossword puzzle shows in Yankee Stadium, 1928 Democratic and Republican party platforms issued in the shape of crossword puzzles, model bathrooms decorated in black and white crossword tiles and the like—it wasn't for lack of interest. Detractors notwithstanding, it was estimated that there were ten million crossword fans in the United States alone.

How did a puzzle command the attention of so many different people so rapidly? While more and more Americans had steadily become puzzle fans over the previous centuries they had never reacted so passionately to any prior puzzle. Analyzing the craze, it is possible to see that like a chemical reaction all the elements had been primed for the resultant explosion. Crosswords merely provided the necessary spark.

This was the era of "Coolidge Prosperity" when workers' spending powers increased dramatically. Now people could pursue the pleasurable trivialities which had formerly been off limits to them. Ever on the lookout for new fads, they had focused their attention on speakeasys, the Charleston, bobbed hair and buying their first car. The crossword was the first intellectual vehicle they adopted in their emulation of the upper classes. For it was only after the intelligentsia of the day em-

The cartoonist's depiction of a crossword-crazy world in 1925 was not so farfetched. When the cartoon appeared, it seemed as if the whole world was mesmerized by crosswords. People who admitted to a noncrossword life risked ostracism from their peers.

THAT GUILTIEST FEELING   by BRIGGS

SUGGESTION TO HOTELS

A CROSSWORD PUZZLE PAD AT THE TELEPHONE IN EACH ROOM WILL SAVE WALL PAPER AND INCREASE PATIENCE OF PATRONS

FOR CAR BELONGING TO CROSS-WORD PUZZLE FAN.

braced the puzzle as a socially acceptable pastime that the masses followed suit.

The crossword had all the necessary elements conducive to becoming a national craze: the cost element was minimal or had already been expended in the purchase of a newspaper where crosswords now appeared; there were no complicated rules; and neither manual dexterity nor unusual equipment was a requisite. These factors, coupled with the higher level of education achieved by the masses, paved the way for the unprecedented growth of the fad. As an added inducement, the media covered the crossword craze extensively. Crosswords were the topic of news articles and editorial columns, comic strips, cartoons and radio broadcasts. Indicative of the kind of features that were being printed was this dialogue in crossword language excerpted from *The Bookman,* a literary journal:

These cartoons were indicative of the attention given to crosswords by the media. It was almost impossible to pick up a current magazine without seeing some reference to the crossword. The cumulative effect of such extensive coverage was a craze that completely engulfed the United States.

Mrs. W. "What is that you're working at, my dear?"

Mrs. F. "I'm tatting Joe's initials on his moreen vest. Are you making that ebon garment for yourself?"

Mrs. W. "Yea. Just a black dress for everyday. Henry says I look rather naif in black."

Mrs. F. "Well, perhaps; but it's a bit too anile for me. Give me something in indigo or, say, ecru."

Mrs. W. "Quite right. There is really no neb in such solemn vestments."

Mrs. F. "Stet."

79

Commuters were and still are some of the most loyal crossword fans. Many trains provided dictionaries for their crossword travelers precisely so scenes like this wouldn't happen.

Naturally, as with any fad, the crossword craze had to taper off. When it did, the aftermath found millions of fans loyally devoted to a daily crossword puzzle in their favorite newspaper. Every subsequent generation has produced new crossword devotees and it is still the crossword that prevails in almost every newspaper and puzzle magazine published today. What are the intrinsic features of this puzzle that enable it not only to survive but to reign in splendor?

There are several distinctive characteristics of the crossword that account for its success. Visually, crosswords appeal to the disciplined part of our psyche. The grid, with its symmetrical black and white squares, is always orderly. Furthermore, interlocking clues enable us to travel from one part of the puzzle to another, yet if some definitions temporarily elude us we can always go on to easier ones in a different part of the puzzle. There's no regimented beginning or middle, but the end result is always a completed grid.

80

Margaret Farrar, who as crossword editor for *The New York World* and *The New York Times,* is often referred to as the *belle dame* of puzzles, feels that crossword solving appeals to people because it enables them to escape from their problems in a mentally stimulating manner. "A person can't worry about paying the rent if he's concerned with finding the answer to 7-down." Increased vocabulary skills and facility with spelling are merely secondary by-products that may develop as a result of the crossword habit; they are by no means the prime reason for the initial addiction.

Perhaps the greatest appeal of crosswords lies in the feeling of accomplishment generated by its completion, for the finished diagram represents a task attempted, attacked and achieved. In our increasingly compartmentalized world, how many tasks do we engage in that have such a beginning, middle and an end?

Crosswords are found in practically every country today. However, nowhere did the crossword take on so distinctive a form as the one that developed in England.

The British-style crossword is more of a distant cousin than a sibling to the American type. The crossword grid consists of a

One of the side effects of crossword solving is an increased vocabulary.

CROSS WORDS IN LONDON

FIRST LADY: "You rotund, decangular, eolithic, ferruginous, neuropathic cassowary, you!"

SECOND LADY: "Blimey, you don't 'arf fancy your blinkin' langwidge since you've bin doin' cross-word puzzles, don't yer?"
— *The Humorist* (London).

symmetrical diagram with black and white squares, but therein the similarity ends. In an American-type puzzle all the letters interlock with other letters; in other words, an across letter is also found in a down word. In the British type there are more unkeyed letters than keyed letters. This means that if you can't figure out a horizontal word there may not be a letter from a vertical word to assist you.

However, the major difference between the two puzzles lies in the clues. American clues are predominantly definition-type where one's knowledge of factual data is being tested, while British puzzles are based on cryptic clues. These clues depend on ingenious twists of words meant to carry the solver on a circuitous solving path. For example, in an American puzzle *smart* might be defined as "intelligent." In a cryptic clue the definition might read "old vehicles when reversing are brisk." Each cryptic clue is in itself an enigma.

Three outstanding English constructors were mainly responsible for raising the level of British crosswords to the high intellectual plane they now occupy. All were brilliant scholars, well versed in philosophy and the classics, and chose to operate under clever noms-de-plume befitting the cunning manner of their puzzles. Torquemada, Afrit and Ximenes—Powys Mather, Alistair Ferguson Ritchie and Derrick Somerset Macnutt, respectively—each put his own particular stamp on the puzzles he constructed.

Torquemada began constructing puzzles for *The Observer* in 1926. He believed that crossword puzzles were split into two groups, the highbrow puzzles for detectives and the lowbrow puzzles for defectives! He devoted his life to constructing cryptic clues for the former group. His definitions were often written in verse and many of them required specialized knowledge of literature.

The vehicle for Afrit's genius was *The Listener*. His clues were scrupulously fair and his coinage of the maxim "You need not mean what you say, but you must say what you mean" is still adhered to by most British constructors today. His clues were often not factual *per se*, but would give all the appropriate information for the answer to be deciphered.

Ximenes was a disciple of Torquemada's but incorporated more of Afrit's philosophy into his definitions. He used every opportunity to utilize humor in his clues and became well known to the freelance contributors to his *Observer* puzzle column as a result of his witty and complimentary notes to them.

One really works hard when solving a cryptic crossword for the clues involve anagrams, riddles, enigmas, transpositions, hidden words and other digressive tactics. For the uninitiated the clues might as well be written in Greek, so difficult are they to decipher. However, after an explanatory answer is provided, you'll be ready to applaud the ingenuity that went into the construction of each and every clue.

Cryptic clues consist of two parts, a literal definition of the word plus a description of its composition. For example, "evokes" might be clued as "calls out what's correct in short in women generally." A breakdown of the clue reveals that "calls out" defines evokes; "what's correct in short" represents OK; "women generally" refers to Eve; and "in" tells the solvers to place OK within Eves.

This is the type of circuitous reasoning that cryptic solvers employ as they attack British-style crosswords. In an anagram-type example, "noted works in a prose version" is answered by "operas," which is arrived at by rearranging "a prose." The fact that the clue is also literally correct adds to its cleverness. It takes a great deal of practice before one becomes adept at solving cryptic puzzles. However, the ego satisfaction that one feels after completing a cryptic puzzle is a powerful stimulant.

British puzzle constructors bemoan the fact that American puzzles are so jejune with their definition-oriented clues. On the other hand, few American puzzlists can make heads or tails out of the English puzzles. It appears as if each country is pleased with its own crossword style and has no intention of shifting gears. In the final analysis, the fact that the two major types of crosswords are distinctly different from each other is inconsequential. What is important to recognize is that many kinds of people are addicted to a crossword of some type or another.

The crossword has had so much impact on the indoor pastime scene for over half a century that it cannot be summarily dismissed as just another puzzle. It is a unique sociological phenomenon and should be recognized as such. First, it is the only puzzle that has ever attracted such a broad range of people to its ranks. Easy crosswords meant to be solved in ten minutes or less attract a certain segment of the population; crosswords composed entirely of arcane definitions necessitating extensive research have their own adherents; and there are millions of people who will spend their time only on cryptic crosswords. In between these extremes are a myriad of variations each appealing to different levels of intellect.

Secondly, crosswords have changed dramatically since their inception, yet have remained essentially the same. The interlocking grid of symmetrical black and white squares still exists. Gone, however, are the two-letter words, unkeyed letters (in American puzzles) and stuffy dictionary definitions that characterized the crosswords of the 1920s. Crosswords today use very sophisticated clues. Multiple word phrases are very common; clues rely more on word play than literal interpretations;

foreign and obsolete words are kept to a minimum and thematic crosswords comprise most of the weekend puzzle fare.

Thirdly, there is a vast number of people who depend on crosswords as a therapeutic tool. For these people the crossword is a necessary part of their day and the even tempo of their lives is disrupted when they don't have access to their favorite crossword. When Margaret Farrar was crossword editor for *The New York Times,* fans would often write to her of their unhappiness when they didn't receive their copy of the paper due to a severe storm, strike or other unforeseen event. During one especially debilitating snowstorm when service to rural areas was completely cut off, a nurse at a hospital in one of the affected areas wrote to Mrs. Farrar and told her that a patient's recovery was in jeopardy unless she received a copy of the answers to a previous puzzle. It seemed that this patient was recuperating through solving *The Times* crossword. Needless to say, the answers were hurriedly dispatched. In an uncertain world crosswords represent a stabilizing influence.

Fourth and foremost, the crossword has met the challenge of all the innovations of the twentieth century for people's leisure time and has held its own in spite of the competition. A 1974 Gallup Poll found that approximately 27 percent of the population does crosswords and that they outrank other indoor sports such as Monopoly, chess, checkers, etc.

Crosswords show no signs of ever becoming extinct. They're an amusing, inexpensive and challenging way to enjoy oneself and will undoubtedly retain their position as one of the all-time favorite indoor pastimes.

PUZZLE PROMO

PUZZLES IN CONTESTS & ADVERTISING

Puzzles are eye catching. They call attention to their presence and lure readers to them for closer examination. Astute promoters have recognized the visual and participatory appeal of puzzles and have used them extensively in publicity drives and advertising campaigns.

Newspapers have often instituted puzzle contests as a means of substantially increasing their circulation. Although the bulk of the new readership has fallen off at the contest's end, the net increase in revenue has been sufficient to sustain use of puzzle contests as promotional gimmicks.

Picture contests first appeared in newspapers early in the twentieth century, and since then the *modus operandi* of all puzzle contests has been to use deceptively simple puzzles at the outset of the competition to capture as many readers as possible. Once the contestants are hooked on the contest, the puzzles become progressively harder until all but the most intrepid players are unable to solve the final puzzles. The prizes are often quite substantial and well worth racking one's brains over. Here are some of the early contests and the grand prizes they offered:

SPONSOR	GRAND PRIZE
Boston Globe, 1912	$2,000
Cleveland News, 1912	$6,000 bungalow
Los Angeles Times, 1912	$1,750 automobile
Pittsburgh Sun, 1913	$500 and $635 piano
Denver Times, 1913	$1000

The pictures were often difficult to decipher in these contests because so many different interpretations were possible. Puzzle-solving handbooks were published to aid contestants in their quest for the lucrative prizes. An examination of the correct answers to picture clues taken from actual contests shows that puzzlers had to be on the same interpretive wave length as the contest designer if they wanted to win those grand prizes:

PICTURE CLUE	PUZZLE ANSWER
Death of a king	The royal end
From 17 to 30	Thirteen

Match gone out	**The light that failed**
Brunette between two blonds	**Between the lights**
Map of Mexico	**Beyond the border**
Mother trying trousers	
on Gerald	**Fitzgerald**

When the crossword mania hit the world in the 1920s, crossword contests became exceedingly popular. These puzzles were so demanding that often there was no clear-cut winner at the end. This is what happened when *The Daily News* in England offered a £5,000 first prize for a crossword contest in 1925. Over 100,000 entrants gave the correct answer to the lead-off puzzle, which was relatively simple. The second puzzle was much harder so that as many contestants as possible would be weeded out. Although the third puzzle demanded knowledge of French, Spanish, German, Italian and higher mathematics, 300 competitors achieved a perfect score. The contest promoters made the final puzzle so difficult that not a single contestant was able to solve it correctly. The first prize was shared by a syndicate of London solvers who had the fewest letters wrong. Undoubtedly, there were people who derived pleasure just from being able to complete the puzzle; but the cash incentive was the real lure for most contestants.

Imagine then what substantial prize money could do for a contest in the 1930s, during the Great Depression. At any point in time a $100,000 first prize would be tempting. But during the depression the appeal of such a huge sum of money caused millions of Americans to become obsessed with a puzzle contest. The Old Gold Rebus Contest of 1937 has to be ranked as the most famous puzzle contest of all time for several reasons: it drew the largest response in terms of numbers of contestants; the cash prize awarded was extraordinary for the time; it received more publicity than any other puzzle contest; a clerical staff of close to 1,000 people was needed to handle all the responses; and it provided over $1 million in earnings to the post office simply for delivering the entries.

On January 25, 1937, the P. Lorillard Company, makers of Old Gold cigarettes, declared in 350 newspapers across the country that it was starting a rebus puzzle contest at the end of which $200,000 in prize money would be divided among 1,000 winners. A grand prize of $100,000 was to go to one lucky person and 999 others would share the remaining $100,000. The contest would be spread over a period of fifteen weeks, and there would be six rebuses to solve per week. Contestants had to mail in their entries weekly, accompanied by three wrappers from Old Gold cigarettes.

The contest obviously struck a responsive chord in the American public. By the May 15 deadline, 2 million people had mailed in 90 answers apiece along with 90 million Old Gold wrappers for which they had paid $13.5 million. However, numbers alone don't tell the complete story. For the contest affected many aspects of American life in a totally unexpected manner. First, the impact on the public libraries was not only extensive, but totally disruptive. In their frenzy to obtain the correct answers to the rebus puzzles, patrons literally attacked their local libraries and put such a strain on their reference facilities that the libraries were forced to rethink their attitudes toward increased attendance. Because of the acute competition for the enormous first prize, there was many a contestant who when he or she found the answer they were looking for in an encyclopedia or dictionary, would tear out the appropriate page, thus preventing someone else from obtaining the needed material. In order to survive, libraries were forced to curtail some of their services. The New York Public Library had to remove several books from circulation and post signs stating, "Dictionaries, encyclopedias and other works of reference are not provided for use in connection with puzzles or contests of any kind." Normally libraries would have been delighted at the increased patronage, but the assault on their books was just too much to accept.

Second, the sales of tipster sheets became a profitable sideline business. Approximately 50,000 people bought answers worked out by others; prices ranged from 10¢ to $15.00. Although the authors of these sheets promised "no guarantee," contestants were still willing to invest money in other people's puzzle-solving skills.

Third, the sales of Old Gold cigarettes increased by 70 percent in the first four months of 1937 over a comparable period in 1936. Although millions of people changed back to their accustomed brands afterwards, the popularity of the contest made Old Gold the most widely talked about cigarette campaign in 1937.

The creator of this contest was F. Gregory Hartswick, one of the three original crossword editors; the Publishers Service Company was the contest promoter who orchestrated the newspaper campaign. Each puzzle was a cartoon that was supposed to represent the name of a person. Every element in the cartoon was a possible clue: the words spoken by the characters, the background pictures, the entire scene, synonyms for anything contained in the cartoon were all carefully constructed to represent syllables of the answer. Contestants had from twelve to twenty names to choose from. In order to ensure that one, and only one, name represented the correct solution, college girls were hired to methodically dissect all the puzzles. The first puz-

LEFT The puzzles used in the Old Gold Rebus Contest were methodically constructed from rough sketches to completed cartoons.

RIGHT Each puzzle in the Old Gold Rebus Contest was analyzed in detail to ascertain that only one answer could be correct.

zles were fairly simple but became increasingly difficult as the contest progressed. At the end of the fifteen weeks, 54,000 people had answered all 90 rebuses correctly, and were still in the running. Hartswick and his staff had to create 90 new puzzles (which they felt were the most difficult they had ever designed), and these were mailed out to the contestants as tiebreakers. They were given ten days to figure them out. When 9,000 people were still viable contestants after completing the second set of rebuses, the promoters ceased using puzzles to determine a winner. The lucky grand prize winner, a naval cadet, was chosen because of his writing ability in the final tiebreaker, an essay entitled "The increased popularity of Old Gold cigarettes in my community as a result of the Old Gold contest."

Was the contest worth the $2 million Lorillard spent on it

($1,200,000 for advertising, $200,000 for prizes and $600,000 for clerical and other expenses)? Although that amount is staggering by 1937 standards, the answer has to be an unqualified Yes! Millions of people were entertained in a depressing depression year; almost 1,000 people were hired temporarily as puzzle verifiers and clerical workers, providing a much needed source of income during this period of high unemployment; another 1,000 people won welcomed cash prizes; and the publicity generated by the frenzy the puzzle caused couldn't be purchased at any price. In terms of numbers, entertainment, excitement and mental stimulation, no other contest has ever matched the Old Gold competition.

Whenever a puzzle contest captured the fancy of a large populace it was the libraries that bore the brunt of the public's quest for the money prizes. Crowds of people, many of whom had never set foot in a library before, would literally invade the reference area in search of the correct solutions. Some librarians welcomed these new patrons because they felt it their duty to serve the public. Others, however, just couldn't cope with such large numbers of people in so short a period of time. Some contestants undoubtedly learned how to use reference materials while researching answers to puzzle contests, but many others were clearly nuisances to the staffs of many a library. The librarians in a Los Angeles library in late 1940 decided to protect their reference books by solving puzzle contest answers themselves and posting them for their readers. The response was very mixed: some puzzlers were overjoyed at this new library "service"; others were furious, for they felt that solvers should do the work themselves. The librarians had actually resorted to the service in self-defense after an unruly crowd searching for the answer to a puzzle contest had to be dispersed by the police.

Not all puzzle contests required such extensive ferreting out of obscure facts. Some promoters have used the Bible as fertile subject matter for contests. A 1955 *Herald Tribune* contest revolved around 54 scrambled letter puzzles representing persons, places, tribes and geographical features mentioned in the Bible. The first prize was $15,000 for the winner and $7,500 for the winner's church.

Although there are still puzzle contests in newspapers, the majority of today's contests are sponsored by organizations specifically set up to conduct contest promotions. Specialized contest magazines or direct-mail solicitations inform prospective participants of current contests. Contestants are usually required to submit a fee ranging from $1 to $20 along with each entry. In effect, these entry fees are providing the pool from which the promoter obtains the money needed for the cash prizes. The first puzzles in most of these contests are so ridiculously easy that a young child can solve them. Of course, puzzles like this are merely the bait to lure prospective entrants into the contest. Naturally, when a puzzle is so simple that thousands of people will all obtain the correct answers, subsequent tiebreaker puzzles are needed. Each puzzle becomes increasingly harder until the final puzzle, demanding the utmost concentration, patience and skill, is reached.

Promoting puzzle contests has evolved into a profitable business for contest organizations. Although no figures are available, it is estimated that millions of dollars are exchanged in puzzle contesting each year. With such large sums of money at stake the entrepreneurial spirit of many a puzzler has been kindled and puzzle-solving methodology has become a business in itself. Professional puzzle solvers who have mastered the art of deciphering the many varied contests on the market offer their

Introductory puzzles tend to be exceedingly easy.

90

skills to would-be winners. Through a thorough analysis and dissection of puzzle contests these pros have developed quasi-scientific methods to increase one's chances of winning. Some of the things that they advocate are:

—Using a wide array of reference materials such as dictionaries, gazetteers, atlases, picture dictionaries and quotation books.
—Entering as many puzzle contests as often as possible.
—Organizing scrapbooks of contests, winning solutions, clues, etc., because many puzzles have been known to be repeated over the years.
—Subscribing to puzzle contest newsletters to keep abreast of the latest contests and to gain valuable solving hints.
—Purchasing some of the solvers' manuals on the market.
—Enrolling in puzzle-solving correspondence courses.

Without these aids it is difficult for a novice to compete adequately in puzzle contests. Although the preliminary puzzles are overly simple in order to whet the contestants' appetites, the later puzzles in a contest are often constructed around such obscure data that inexperienced and unequipped solvers stand little or no chance of winning any of the prizes.

The puzzles used by promoters are of diverse types, with the pictorial variety being most prevalent. Rebus puzzles necessitating the addition and subtraction of words to form an answer word use pictures of obscure objects as clues. In the example pictured below, the answer CATT, could only be derived if a

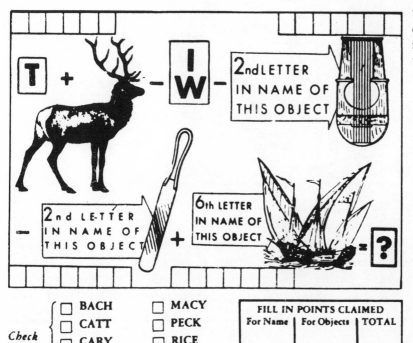

The correct answer, CATT, is obtained as follows: T + WAPITI − IW − I − P + C.

contestant knew the names of the pictured objects. In order of appearance, they are WAPITI, CITHARA, SPATULA and FELUCCA —hardly words in one's everyday vocabulary. The professional solver, of course, has access to a picture dictionary and will stand a good chance of cracking the puzzle.

In a cartoon-type puzzle the logic used by the constructor is often circuitous, so that if contestants don't learn to reason along the same lines they stand no chance of deciphering such puzzles. Every word and picture in this type of puzzle is a possible clue. In the example below the correct solution, SAMUEL BUCKLEY, is arrived at through the following dissection procedure:

> **Try means to essay; phonetically essay equals S A: combined with mule it becomes Samule or *SAMUEL*. A synonym for haul is *BUCK* and another for grassy plain is *LEA*; combined these become Bucklea or *BUCKLEY*.**

To solve these contests one must break down all the suggested answers, syllable by syllable, and search out each component of every word to see if it is included in the diagram. If *every* syllable of an answer cannot be found in the cartoon, that answer has to be eliminated.

In a word-frame puzzle contest the contestant actually constructs a puzzle. Each letter of the alphabet is given a numerical value by the puzzle creator. The contestant must fill in the puzzle grid with interlocking words aiming to reach the highest score possible. The illustration on page 94 shows how a pro would solve this puzzle. The sponsor allowed intersecting letters a value that was three times their normal worth and the contestant utilized the highest scoring letters at the intersection. An overwhelming percentage of the words used are arcane; thus

OPPOSITE   A picture dictionary is a helpful aid to professional contesters. Here is a typical page.

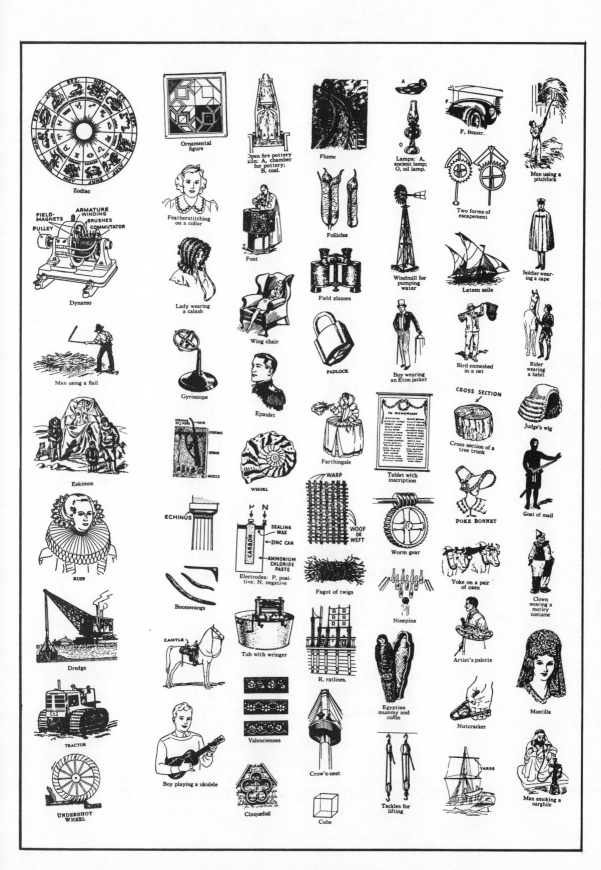

Zodiac

Ornamental figure

Open fire pottery kiln: A, chamber for pottery; B, coal.

Flume

Lamps: A, ancient lamp; O, oil lamp.

F, fender.

Man using a pitchfork

FIELD-MAGNETS, ARMATURE WINDING, BRUSHES, COMMUTATOR, PULLEY

Dynamo

Featherstitching on a collar

Font

Follicles

Windmill for pumping water

Two forms of escapement

Lateen sails

Soldier wearing a cape

Man using a flail

Lady wearing a calash

Gyroscope

Wing chair

Field glasses

PADLOCK

Boy wearing an Eton jacket

Bird enmeshed in a net

Rider wearing a habit

Eskimos

OPENING OF PORE, HAIR, EPIDERMIS, DERMIS, MUSCLE

Epaulet

WHORL

Farthingale

IN MEMORIAM

Tablet with inscription

CROSS SECTION

Cross section of a tree trunk

Judge's wig

RUFF

ECHINUS

Boomerangs

Electrodes: P, positive; N, negative

SEALING WAX, CARBON, ZINC CAN, AMMONIUM CHLORIDE PASTE

WARP, WOOF OR WEFT

Fagot of twigs

Worm gear

POKE BONNET

Goat of mail

Dredge

CANTLE

Tub with wringer

R, ratlines.

Ninepins

Yoke on a pair of oxen

Clown wearing a motley costume

TRACTOR

Boy playing a ukulele

Valenciennes

Crow's-nest

Egyptian mummy and coffin

Artist's palette

Nutcracker

Mantilla

UNDERSHOT WHEEL

Cinquefoil

Cube

Tackles for lifting

YARDS

Man smoking a narghile

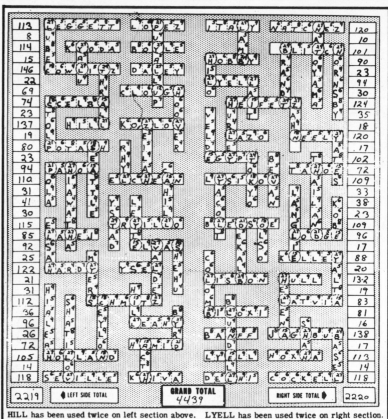

A completed word frame puzzle used in a contest. The solver must continually jiggle words in order to obtain the highest possible score.

HILL has been used twice on left section above.   LYELL has been used twice on right section.

Values of Letters: A-5   B-8   C-6   D-7   E-5   F-8   G-5   H-9   I-5   J-8   K-6   L-9   M-6
O-6   P-7   Q-8   R-4   S-6   T-8   U-4   V-9   W-4   X-9   Y-9   Z-9   N-6

Count each letter once. Intersecting letters are worth triple the above value. Additional words that can be used are: XANTHUS VANDALS LEYTE ZUKHOV DALEY ELFELD LHASA SCHMIDT FERNDALE JOHN DVINSK LAIT UTRECHT VELDE ZEILAH LYSIKOV VINA KITAB HARTLE HONSHU LOZLOV TOKYO CHILE HEIFETZ KHARKHOV KELLEY LATVIA SHARKEY BEVAN LYNDEN PABST HARDY. With these extra words, see if you can improve or increase the score. Shift words around. You can do it, if you try.

the use of an unabridged dictionary is almost mandatory. A great deal of time goes into solving this type of puzzle for words must continuously be juxtaposed until the highest score is reached.

Contest promoters have been extremely creative in the variety of puzzles they have devised. There are literally hundreds of types of puzzles used in contests. However, in spite of the myriad of contests sponsored in any one year, true puzzlers— those whose main pleasure is derived from the joy of solving— shun these contests. These people feel that puzzle contesting takes advantage of a puzzler's passion for solving by offering lucrative cash prizes, which, in reality, cannot be solved by just any puzzler. One must have mastered the tricks of the trade to win the valuable prizes. However, for puzzle aficionados who want to take the time to learn the secrets of successful solving, the puzzle contest route may well be worth pursuing. The main pitfall to avoid is to be taken in by unscrupulous promoters who

94

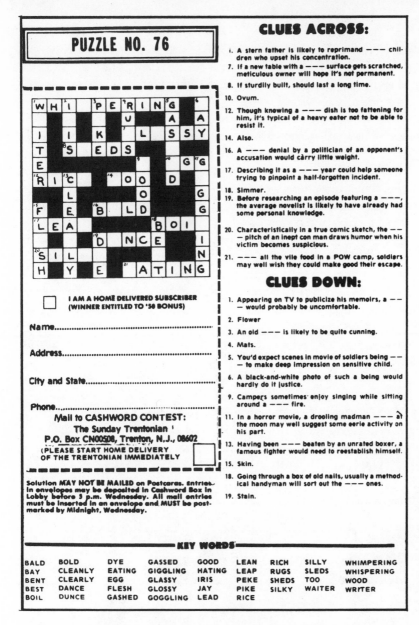

PUZZLE NO. 76

Crossword grid (partially filled):

```
W H I _ P E R I N G
    K     L   S S Y
  _ S E D S       G _ G
        _ O O D     G
    L     O         G
F _ E A   B _ D   B O I
    D N C E         I N
S I L     _         N
H Y E   _ A T I N G
```

CLUES ACROSS:

1. A stern father is likely to reprimand ——— children who upset his concentration.
7. If a new table with a ——— surface gets scratched, meticulous owner will hope it's not permanent.
8. If sturdily built, should last a long time.
10. Ovum.
12. Though knowing a ——— dish is too fattening for him, it's typical of a heavy eater not to be able to resist it.
14. Also.
16. A ——— denial by a politician of an opponent's accusation would carry little weight.
17. Describing it as a ——— year could help someone trying to pinpoint a half-forgotten incident.
18. Simmer.
19. Before researching an episode featuring a ———, the average novelist is likely to have already had some personal knowledge.
20. Characteristically in a true comic sketch, the ——— pitch of an inept con man draws humor when his victim becomes suspicious.
21. ——— all the vile food in a POW camp, soldiers may well wish they could make good their escape.

CLUES DOWN:

1. Appearing on TV to publicize his memoirs, a ——— would probably be uncomfortable.
2. Flower
3. An old ——— is likely to be quite cunning.
4. Mats.
5. You'd expect scenes in movie of soldiers being ——— to make deep impression on sensitive child.
6. A black-and-white photo of such a being would hardly do it justice.
9. Campers sometimes enjoy singing while sitting around a ——— fire.
11. In a horror movie, a drooling madman ——— at the moon may well suggest some eerie activity on his part.
13. Having been ——— beaten by an unrated boxer, a famous fighter would need to reestablish himself.
15. Skin.
18. Going through a box of old nails, usually a methodical handyman will sort out the ——— ones.
19. Stain.

Only a few letters are needed to complete this puzzle and win a lucrative prize. The choice of letters, however, is dependent on one's ability to interpret the clues correctly. Copyright © 1977 United Features Syndicate. (*See* Picture Answers, 14.)

KEY WORDS

BALD	BOLD	DYE	GASSED	GOOD	LEAN	RICH	SILLY	WHIMPERING
BAY	CLEANLY	EATING	GIGGLING	HATING	LEAP	RUGS	SLEDS	WHISPERING
BENT	CLEARLY	EGG	GLASSY	IRIS	PEKE	SHEDS	TOO	WOOD
BEST	DANCE	FLESH	GLOSSY	JAY	PIKE	SILKY	WAITER	WRITER
BOIL	DUNCE	GASHED	GOGGLING	LEAD	RICE			

never pay out prize money to the winners. Unfortunately, such organizations do exist and to protect oneself it's best to deal only with reputable sponsors.

The puzzle contests found in newspapers are frequently constructed by major syndicates. Sealed contest answers are deposited with a reputable bank so that the newspapers themselves do not know the answers in advance. At the end of the contest the answers are opened and the prize money is divided among the correct entries. Partially solved crosswords are one of the most popular types of puzzles for such contests. While the puzzle may appear simple at first glance, it is actually rather difficult. The trick is to choose one correct answer from two words which are spelled exactly alike except for one letter. Thus each word in the clue becomes vital. Because so many of the answers in a puzzle like this depend on a contestant's ability to interpret the clues in the exact manner as the constructor, these contests are not easy to win.

As we have seen in earlier chapters, puzzles play a more pervasive role in society than is apparent at first glance. People who ignore the crossword in their newspaper and thus feel they're immune to puzzles might, however, respond when puzzles are presented in an extraordinary manner. This is the premise used by advertisers and public relations managers who have incorporated puzzles into their campaigns. Thematic puzzles based on the advertiser's product or service are created by specialized puzzle constructors. An example of a puzzle created for The New York Telephone Company by Jesse Jacobs, such a specialist, is shown below. The message, "HAVE YOU ORDERED YOUR PRINCESS PHONES?" will undoubtedly have more impact on the target audience than a traditional ad because of the reader's active response to it via his or her solving of the crossword.

Numerous other advertisers have found the subliminal use of clues relating to their product to be most effective. In 1970 Macy's ran a two-page crossword puzzle in *The New York Times* and offered prizes for the correct solution. References to

A specialized puzzle for telephone customers.

Macy's products and services were sprinkled abundantly throughout the puzzle, and the enthusiastic response to the ad, as measured by the number of completed puzzles sent in, justified its high cost—space costs alone were $16,000.

Public relations managers have recognized the power of puzzles and used thematic crosswords in company publications and puzzle contests for employees. Invariably these special puzzles have been well received because people like the idea of becoming involved. And when puzzlers are familiar with the company or product being spotlighted, their appetite for that company's product is further whetted by the puzzle.

Not all advertisers want to include an entire puzzle in an ad. Sometimes just the mere suggestion of a puzzle motif in a well-designed ad is sufficient to make that ad stand out among the other ads vying for the reader's attention, as in the clever advertisement below (left), which plays on the analogy between solving a crossword and solving a decorating problem.

Rebuses are used to carry messages in a clever manner. The eye-catching flyer pictured below (right) was created by a film lab, dependent on mail order business. An ad like this is unusual because the use of pictures instead of words is a novelty;

LEFT   A partial puzzle draws attention to an advertisement.

RIGHT   Rebus advertisements are hard to ignore. This one was created by a mail-order film laboratory.

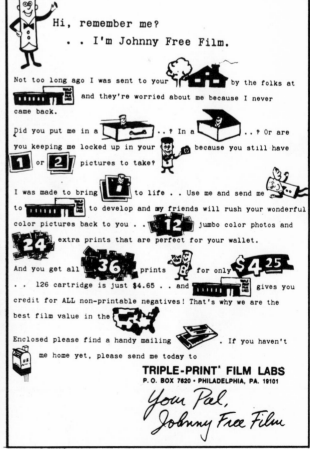

the reader feels that he or she has to decipher the message and respond accordingly.

The purpose of advertising is to attract the attention of a target audience to a message about one's product in the hopes that they will purchase it. The most successful advertisers are those whose creative efforts are rewarded with increased sales of their product. While a puzzle in an ad is no guarantee that the public will purchase the product, the reader will almost certainly be drawn to it. Puzzles are difficult to ignore, for they flaunt their solvability and challenge the reader to attack them.

FAMOUS PUZZLE PEOPLE

The familiar squared diagram of the crossword which many people incorrectly equate with *all* puzzles leads many to believe that puzzle construction lies somewhere between "connecting the dots" and "painting by numbers." Although puzzle forms do tend to be more or less standardized, the content of each puzzle is original. Each grid is a symmetrical design based on the particular words in the puzzle, and each design is a unique arrangement of words and spaces. Clues are now much more than dictionary definitions and the constructor has unlimited leeway to present his definitions in his own individual style. Moreover, in addition to the crossword, there is a myriad of puzzle varieties, each a product of an inventive mind. And like any other creative person, the puzzle constructor reveals much about himself and his philosophy of life through his output.

Puzzle history has been shaped by several exceptional constructors who have poured their creativity and individuality into their puzzles and have amassed loyal followings of puzzle solvers. Although there have been many people who composed puzzles for fun and/or profit, space limitations permit only a handful of them to be discussed here in any detail.

Sam Loyd

Dubbed the "prince of puzzle makers," Sam Loyd was the most flamboyant and prolific constructor. He was one of the few individuals to derive most of his income from puzzles. Born in 1841, he studied to be an engineer. He had always enjoyed amusing himself with puzzles and, as a pastime, he started to produce and sell them to newspapers. When he began to make more money from puzzles than from his regular employment, he decided to devote his full energies to puzzling.

Sam Loyd's greatest successes came from the puzzle gimmicks he designed for clients to be used as promotional giveaways. Loyd believed in producing puzzles which appeared so simple that people would feel compelled to solve them. In actuality, solvers would spend hours on his puzzles without being able to figure them out.

Sam Loyd.

Loyd's creative genius was apparent at an early age. He was only seventeen when he invented the "Trick Donkeys" for P. T. Barnum to use as an advertisement for his circus. One of his most famous puzzles, it involved two donkeys and two riders which had to be arranged so that each rider was astride a donkey. The puzzle looked far simpler than it was!

Another of his most famous efforts was "The 14-15 Puzzle," which can still be found in novelty shops today. Many a person will remember spending hours on this puzzle as a child. Fifteen square blocks numbered from 1 to 15 are arranged at random, in a square box capable of holding sixteen such squares. The object is to arrange the numbers serially from 1 to 15. When this puzzle appeared in the 1870s, Loyd offered a prize of $1,000 for the first correct solution, but the money was never claimed. Loyd was unable to patent the puzzle because a "working model" had to be filed along with the patent application. Since the puzzle was mathematically impossible to do, Loyd couldn't produce the necessary prototype. In his *Cyclope-*

To place the two riders on the donkeys it was necessary to first place the donkeys' backs to each other and then lay the riders parallel with the donkeys' backs. This unusual solution was indicative of Loyd's puzzles.

MARSHALL AND BALL'S FAMOUS TRICK DONKEYS.

CUT ON THE LINES AND LAY THE THREE PIECES SO AS TO SHOW THE JOCKEYS RACING

dia of Puzzles, Loyd talks about the impact of this puzzle on the public:

> People became infatuated with the puzzle and ludicrous tales are told of shopkeepers who neglected to open their stores; of a distinguished clergyman who stood under a street lamp all through a wintry night trying to recall the way he had performed the feat. The mysterious feature of the puzzle is that no one seems to be able to recall the sequence of moves whereby they feel sure they succeeded in solving the puzzle. Pilots are said to have wrecked their ships, engineers rush their trains past stations and business generally became demoralized. A famous Baltimore editor tells how he went for his noon lunch and was discovered by his frantic staff long past midnight pushing little pieces of pie around on his plate! Farmers are known to have deserted their plows and I have taken one of such instances as an illustration for this sketch [see illustration below].

Although these anecdotes about people's obsession with "The 14-15 Puzzle" are undoubtedly exaggerated, Loyd did have the uncanny ability to produce novelties which generated intense public attention.

Loyd's "Get off the Earth" puzzle was designed in 1896 as a premium to advertise Bergen Beach, a newly opened resort in New Jersey. Loyd regarded it as his *chef d'oeuvre.* No puzzle has ever generated as much controversy as this one. Although Loyd's weekly puzzle column in *The Brooklyn Daily Eagle* was filled for a year with attempted explanations, no one ever adequately analyzed this spectacular feat of legerdemain.

In Loyd's words, the puzzle consisted of "two concentric pieces of cardboard, fastened together so that the smaller inner one, which was circular, moved slightly backward and forward, on a pivot, producing the mystery. As you looked at them there

The farmer's anguish at his inability to solve this impossible puzzle was echoed by millions of other perplexed puzzlers.

R T H D X X F R D
D N S D N T K N W
L D P R T F R M
L G W D

HERE IS A SOUVENIR from our college days which will interest the juvenile spelling class. It is built upon similar lines to the story of the epitaph upon the walls of the old abbey, which read:

P.RS.V.R.Y.P.RF.CTM.N
.V.RK..PTH.S.PR.C.PTST.N

The dots represent a certain vowel which had faded from the inscription. In the present illustration the college professor of etymology was asked to construct the sentence properly by the introdution of the one vowel.

A REBUS.

My first you hear its sullen roar
When wandering by the ocean's shore;
My second in the gambler's art
Hath played no mean or paltry part,
But, fired with sordid thirst to win,
It often aids him in his sin.
My whole is something that is found
Upon the face of all around,
Yet if you take from me my face,
I am a title commonplace.
Cypher Ans. 19, 21, 18, 6, 1, 3, 5.

Why is an acquitted prisoner like a gun? Because he is charged, taken up, and then let off.

Why are horses little needed in the Isle of Wight? Because visitors prefer Cower to Ryde (cows to ride).

Why are bad riddles like a deserted inn keeper? Because there is a host put out and not one guest (guessed).

A Puzzling Verdict.

Here is what we will term a necktie puzzle, wherein the object is to discover a missing word to be placed in the bow, so that by reading it twice as you go around the loop the sentence will be complete. I think the sentence in this case should have been a hempen necktie around the culprit's neck on account of a missing watch which was found in his possession, but by some twist of the law the sentence was defective, so I will ask our young puzzlists to supply the missing wordl so as to make the sentence correct.

Why does a donkey eat thistles? Because he's an ass.

A REBUS.

My first is a color; my second an agreeable exercise; my third an article of clothing, and my whole a celebrated character, dear to the young folks.
Cypher Ans. 18, 5, 4, 18, 9, 4, 9, 14, 7, 8, 15, 15, 4.

A PUZZLE.

Place the same word in the blanks so as to make each line read properly.
1] The———to Fingal's cave would———the visitor.
2. The Arabs sometimes——— travelers in the———.
3. To select———sometimes——— a writer to annoyance.
4. To excuse donating they——— to the———.

A CRYPTOGRAM.

E10100010001000 U N 1100 A T X N. Answer: Excommunication.
Take the bees away from something we eat and make it read out loud! Ans. Bread and butter becomes read and utter.

What is the difference between a bottle of medicine and a troublesome boy? One is to be well shaken before taken, the other to be taken and then shaken.

Why is a loaf of bread on the top of the Eiffel Tower like a racehorse? Because it is high bread.

At what time was Adam married? Upon his wedding Eve.

What part of a fish is like the end of a book? Don't you know? Why, the

FIN–IS.

A page from Sam Loyd's *Cyclopedia of Puzzles*.

were thirteen Chinamen plainly pictured. Move the inner card around a little and only twelve Chinamen remained. You couldn't tell what had become of the other Chinaman, try as you would."

Loyd truly mesmerized the public with "Get off the Earth." People were willing to spend hours on the puzzle because it seemed so simple. In reality it was almost impossible to solve.

Loyd's explanation in his newspaper column of "changing a right leg for a left one between the fourth and fifth men" does not sufficiently explain the paradox. Loyd was not really about to divulge the secrets of his trade! A more plausible interpretation, according to some puzzle historians, is that the figures are so adroitly drawn that the thirteen warriors merge into twelve slightly larger warriors and that no one warrior entirely disappears.

Working out of a dusty, cluttered office in Manhattan, Loyd produced thousands of other advertising premiums and puzzles of many, many varieties. The range of his genius was extraordinary and his popularity immense. His puzzle gimmicks were able to generate excitement because they were ingeniously conceived and artistically executed. In addition, the distribution of his puzzles was generally handled by advertisers who had a vested interest in ensuring that the premiums were properly promoted.

Loyd's greatest puzzle starts with 13 Chinese warriors and ends with 12. The task of figuring out which warrior disappears generated heated controversy. Loyd's puzzle column in *The Brooklyn Daily Eagle* was filled for a year with "explanations," none of which were correct.

Lewis Carroll

In contrast to Sam Loyd, whose popularity and income were derived mainly from puzzles, Lewis Carroll is best remembered as something other than a puzzler. *Alice's Adventures in Wonderland* and *Through the Looking-Glass* brought enormous acclaim to Carroll. Yet his puzzle activities, though not so well publicized, were as inventive and amusing as his children's classics.

Charles Lutwidge Dodgson, the shy, stammering lecturer and author of mathematical treatises, was also Lewis Carroll, the witty constructor of games and word puzzles. Carroll in-

103

Lewis Carroll was fond of composing humorous rebus letters to his young friends, who delighted in receiving them. (*See* Picture Answers, 15.)

vented them by the score. Some he submitted to publications, others he included in letters to friends and many he carried around with him in a black bag ready to distribute to eager children whom he would meet on his travels.

When the art of anagramming was again in vogue during the late 1800s, Carroll created several masterpieces which remain as classic examples today. He is responsible for such clever rearrangements as FLIT ON, CHEERING ANGEL for FLORENCE NIGHTINGALE and TENDER NAMES for ENDEARMENTS.

He also invented the game "Doublets," which links two words together by changing one letter at a time in a chain of words. For example, to link HEAD to TAIL, the progression of words would read:

HEAD

HEAL

TEAL

TELL

TALL

TAIL

This game is found today in many puzzle magazines and remains a clever word challenge.

Excerpts from Carroll's diary indicate that he had contemplated combining his love of puzzles with his successful *Alice* books by publishing "a little book of original puzzles etc., which I think of calling *Alice's Puzzle Book*." Although the idea never came to fruition, he did submit a column called "Puzzles from Wonderland" to *Aunt Judy's Magazine* in December 1870. A few examples follow:

> **Dreaming of apples on a wall,**
> **And dreaming often, dear,**
> **I dreamed that, if I counted all,**
> **How many would appear?**

Ten

> **What is most like a bee in May?**
> **"Well, let me think: perhaps—" you say.**
> **Bravo! You're guessing well to-day!**

Maybe

Carroll was fond of forming friendships with little girls, and he would frequently amuse his female friends with acrostics written especially for them, such as this double acrostic on the names of the two Misses Bremer:

Two little girls near London dwell,
More naughtly than I like to tell.

1. Upon the lawn the hoops are seen:			
The balls are rolling on the green.	T	ur	F
2. The Thames is running deep and wide;			
And boats are rowing on the tide.	R	ive	R
3. In winter-time, all in a row,			
The happy skaters come and go.	I	c	E
4. "Papa!" they cry, "Do let us stay!"			
He does not speak, but says they may.	N	o	D
5. "There is a land," he says, "my dear,			
Which is too hot to skate, I fear."	A	fric	A

Carroll's puzzle activities were more personal than any of the other famous puzzlers. Constructing puzzles was his unique way of showing affection for his friends.

Margaret Farrar

People associate modern-day puzzles primarily with the crossword, a craze beginning in the mid and late 1920s and spreading like wildfire all over the world to become an established form of entertainment. Many people come to mind in considering the development of Arthur Wynne's modest brainchild—first Word-Cross (in 1913), then Crossword—but in the United States (the British scene is a different story) the name most often mentioned is Margaret Farrar, puzzle editor/constructor/aficionado for almost sixty years.

Mrs. Farrar, nee Petherbridge, was one of the famous triumvirate responsible for launching the crossword craze. As puzzle editor of *The New York World, The New York Times* and all of Simon and Schuster's lengthy puzzle series, she has turned a "completely accidental career" into a life's work of puzzle editing. It was under her long-term guidance that crosswords evolved from the emu-gnu-roc variety to the sophisticated game of word play that is so widely popular today.

Mrs. Farrar was a neophyte in the puzzle game when she was entrusted with the crossword column at *The World,* but her interest wasn't long in developing. As the puzzle catapulted into the national spotlight and then became ensconced as one of the prime American pastimes, Mrs. Farrar's expertise appealed to increasing audiences. She says modestly but emphatically, however, that pioneering constructors were responsible for a major share in perfecting the art of crossword making.

Simon and Schuster, quick to capitalize on their first success in 1924, continues to publish crossword books. Margaret Farrar has edited every one of their series and is currently working on the latest edition. She was also the first puzzle editor for *The New York Times,* which inaugurated its Sunday puzzle on February 15, 1942. The apocryphal story is that when the editor of *The Times* realized that he was purchasing *The Herald Tribune* for its crossword, he decided to include a crossword in his own newspaper. Originally the crossword was intended to be a forum for current events and was supposed to be primarily a news-oriented puzzle. Gradually, the puzzle evolved into a stimulating topical crossword with a loyal following of millions. When *The Times* started its daily crossword series in September, 1950, Mrs. Farrar's workload increased accordingly, but the puzzles remained at the same high caliber as those in the Sunday edition.

Crossword constructors have found in Mrs. Farrar an editor very receptive to new ideas. Some of the changes that have been initiated through the collaboration of constructor and editor have been the elimination of two-letter words and unkeyed let-

Margaret Farrar.

ters and the inclusion of multiple-word phrases, quotations, proper names and foreign words.

Mrs. Farrar's involvement with crosswords encompasses more than fifty years and during that time she has undoubtedly influenced millions of people. Because she has always remained accessible to her public, she has had some interesting correspondence and telephone calls from puzzlers. One man wrote asking if *The Times* could save his marriage by printing two copies of the Sunday puzzle. Both he and his wife were avid puzzlers and neither wished to yield the puzzle to the other. Mrs. Farrar suggested that they buy two copies of the paper and donate all but the puzzle page of the second one to a local hospital. Whether they chose to follow her advice or got divorced instead is unknown. In another instance, a woman called asking to have her memory refreshed about a recent puzzle she had solved. In it there had been an unusual word meaning "housewife." When the answer *oikologist* was passed on to her, her thanks were effusive. It seemed that she had wished to use this word on her passport application in the space marked

OCCUPATION. Mrs. Farrar's most heartwarming story of the impact of the crossword on what is essentially an unseen public was the report of a young American couple doing a crossword puzzle while trapped in a stalled cable car below Mt. Blanc. So calm were they and so engrossed in what they were doing that the other imperiled passengers gathered round and they solved the puzzle as a group. The party was rescued with all in good morale!

Mrs. Farrar's mandatory retirement from *The Times* in 1969 generated a flood of letters from her devotees. Perhaps the one that best sums up her influence on the crossword-conscious puzzle fans is the following:

> **To the Editor:**
>
> **I am one of the people whose lives Margaret Farrar has ruined. For nearly twenty years, when I lived in Westchester, I took part in a spirited competition on the commuter train to see who could finish the daily puzzle first. The rule was that you couldn't even peek at it until the train started to move out of 125th Street on its way to Grand Central—an 11-minute trip. You had to stop (and, of course, have the puzzle finished) before the train stopped. I am happy to be able to report that I moved out of the suburbs undefeated.**
>
> **I cite this minor accomplishment not out of immodesty but merely to indicate how faithfully I have trained under her aegis. To the despair of my family and friends, I am a Sunday addict too. And because of all the happy hours I have spent as her disciple, I cannot let her retirement go by without expressing my fervent appreciation for all the challenging pleasure she has given me.**
>
> **E. J. Kahn, Jr., *The New Yorker*, New York, N.Y.**

Torquemada

The Margaret Farrar type of crossword may remain as America's favorite puzzle, but the British version is equally popular in the United Kingdom and associated Commonwealth countries. Its most distinguishing feature is that the clues are all couched in cryptic terminology. The person most responsible for developing this inimitable British style was Powys Mather, better known to his puzzle audience as Torquemada.

When the American crossword first swept through England in 1924, Torquemada was unimpressed with a puzzle that required mere "dictionary definitions." However, the puzzle form itself stuck with him and sometime later he developed his own version of it. His first puzzles were presented to friends for their

Powys Mather alias Torquemada.

amusement. One of these friends happened to be a literary agent, and so it was that these puzzles were ultimately published in the *Saturday Westminster*. Soon afterwards *The Observer* invited Torquemada to contribute puzzles and in 1926 his famous series began its long run. He quickly built up a faithful following of fans who greatly enjoyed the mental stimulation of his puzzles.

Torquemada's puzzles are truly original. The clues are ingenious: they involve much knowledge of poetry and literature, and above all require that a puzzler exercise his brain in non-traditional thought patterns. Examples of some of his unique definitions show how attuned one had to be to his extraordinary way of thinking:

CLUE	ANSWER
The artist has been about cooked with herbs	SAGED
Marriage days	WEDS
We can't honestly say there's no harm in it, but we're glad the French girl's got it	CHARME
Tell the physician to love, and then he's quite often my subject	DRAMA
In off a Longfellow hero; he will not fraternise	STANDISH (Miles Stand-off-ish)

BELOW A typical Torquemada puzzle, virtually impossible for the uninitiated to solve. Only prior experience with other Torquemada puzzles could give one the requisite experience. (*See* Picture Answers, 16.)

Moreover, as can be seen in a complete example of a Torquemada puzzle, there were often many interconnections between the clues so that a finished puzzle was more than a mere assemblage of unrelated words.

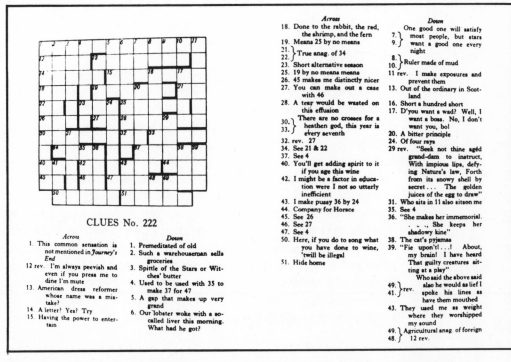

CLUES No. 222

Across

1. This common sensation is not mentioned in *Journey's End*
12 rev. I'm always peevish and even if you press me to dine I'm mute
13. American dress reformer whose name was a mistake?
14. A letter? Yes? Try
15. Having the power to entertain

18. Done to the rabbit, the red, the shrimp, and the fern
19. Means 25 by no means
21.⎫ True anag. of 34
22.⎭
23. Short alternative season
25. 19 by no means means
26. 45 makes me distinctly nicer
27. You can make out a case with 46
28. A tear would be wasted on this effusion
30.⎫ There are no crosses for a heathen god, this year is
33.⎭ every seventh
32. rev. 27
34. See 21 & 22
37. See 4
40. You'll get adding spirit to it if you age this wine
42. I might be a factor in education were I not so utterly inefficient
43. I make pussy 36 by 24
44. Company for Horace
45. See 26
46. See 27
47. See 4
50. Here, if you do to song what you have done to wine, 'twill be illegal
51. Hide home

Down

1. Premeditated of old
2. Such a warehouseman sells groceries
3. Spittle of the Stars or Witches' butter
4. Used to be used with 35 to make 37 for 47
5. A gap that makes up very grand
6. Our lobster woke with a so-called liver this morning. What had he got?

One good one will satisfy
7.⎫ most people, but stars
9.⎭ want a good one every night
8.⎫
10.⎭ Ruler made of mud
11 rev. I make exposures and prevent them
13. Out of the ordinary in Scotland
16. Short a hundred short
17. D'you want a wad? Well, I want a boss. No, I don't want you, bol
20. A bitter principle
24. Of four rays
29 rev. "Seek not thine agéd grand-dam to instruct, With impious lips, defying Nature's law, Forth from its snowy shell by secret . . . The golden juices of the egg to draw"
31. Who sits in 11 also sitson me
35. See 4
36. "She makes her immemorial. . . ., She keeps her shadowy kine"
38. The cat's pyjamas
39. "Fie upon't! . . .! About, my brain! I have heard That guilty creatures sitting at a play"
Who said the above said
49.⎫ also he would as lief I
41.⎭ rev. spoke his lines as have them mouthed
43. They used me as weight where they worshipped my sound
49.⎫ Agricultural anag. of foreign
48.⎭ 12 rev.

Torquemada was especially suited to devoting himself to being the extremely literate puzzle constructor he was for several reasons. First, he had been well educated at Trinity College, Oxford, and was an omnivorous reader. Second, he was in ill health for most of his adult life and unfortunately did not have the physical stamina to fulfill his prime desire to become an author. Third, his personal temperament was compatible with the somewhat isolated life led by puzzle constructors. He shunned large crowds and generally limited his social life to informal gatherings with intimates. His wife was his major confidante, friend and helpmate. She collaborated with him by constructing the puzzle forms from the word lists he compiled. Although his life was brief, Torquemada made a deep impact on the puzzle world.

Elizabeth Kingsley

Elizabeth Kingsley earned her place in the puzzlers' hall of fame by inventing a totally new puzzle, the double-crostic. Unimpressed with the crossword puzzle, she thought that its main detraction was its lack of a "goal." Merely filling words into spaces seemed futile to her and she was determined to invent a "puzzle with a purpose" to elevate puzzle solving to a higher intellectual plane. Thus was born the double-crostic.

The double-crostic consists of two parts: a series of definitions and a puzzle grid blocked out with squares representing words from a quotation. The solver figures out the definitions and then places their letters in the appropriate numbered squares in the grid. When completed, the first letters of all the definitions, when read in order, spell out an author's name and the title of the work. The words in the grid spell out a quotation from this work.

Mrs. Kingsley used the double-crostic format to "heighten an appreciation of fine literature by reviewing English and American poet and prose masters." In 1934, when she compiled a formidable sample of these puzzles, she took them to the editors at *The Saturday Review of Literature*. They were so impressed with them that they instituted a special double-crostic puzzle column which still exists today. Throughout her years as composer of the double-crostic, Mrs. Kingsley rigorously adhered to the high standards she had set for herself. Her puzzles were masterpieces of erudite clues based on literary works. Her philosophy regarding the use of dictionaries and other references was that these were valuable tools and should certainly be used if the solver felt they were necessary. Because so many of her clues were direct quotations from literature, a variety of reference aids was often needed.

Double-Crostics: Number 1

By ELIZABETH S. KINGSLEY

DIRECTIONS

To solve this puzzle, you must guess twenty-five words, the definitions of which are given in the column headed DEFINITIONS. The letters in each word to be guessed are numbered (these numbers appear at the beginning of each definition) and you are thereby able to tell how many letters are in the required word. When you have guessed a word each letter is to be written in the correspondingly numbered square on the puzzle diagram. When the squares are all filled in you will find (by reading from left to right) a quotation from a famous author. Reading up and

down the letters mean nothing! The black squares indicate ends of words; therefore words do not necessarily end at the right side of the diagram.

Either before (preferably) or after placing the letters in their squares you should write the words you have guessed on the blank lines which appear to the right in the column headed WORDS. The initial letters of this list of words spell the name of the author and the title of the piece from which the quotation has been taken.

DEFINITIONS

I. 1-14-23-50-95. A perfume of roses.

II. 145-6-28-90-137. Child's game played with cards and numbers.

III. 97-8-79-146-98-61-75-77-76-32-27-19-133. Light as a feather.

IV. 80-85-60-113-51-58-48. Held in high esteem; worshipped.

V. 81-172-31-84-24-176-65-89. Insubstantial.

VI. 112-45-114-164-149-173-142-36. The business section of a city.

VII. 144-102-2-63. Material for bandages.

VIII. 37-4-66-82-110-116-62. Upholstered backless seat.

IX. 100-106-33-5-122-41-138-69-83-13-162-127. A Russian pianist.

X. 40-59-52-25. A drupe with a single seed.

XI. 135-175-3-73. Movement of the ocean.

XII. 130-43-129-107-111-55-139-47. To alienate.

XIII. 15-121-92-136-101-39. A mighty hunter.

XIV. 167-9-140-46-105. Artless; simple.

XV. 119-54-104-17-153-34. Hebrew God.

XVI. 134-64-128-168-16-30. Flat, dark image.

XVII. 155-125-78-148-143-165-158-56. Prejudiced (compound).

XVIII. 12-96-120-11-7-170-150-21-68-174. Significant, unusual.

XIX. 87-141-171-161-67-20-10-126. Not propitious.

XX. 177-99-152-163-108-115. Member of the tribe of Levi.

XXI. 42-88-26-159-49-91. Doodle dandy.

XXII. 22-71-151-118-131-147-38-94-160-29. Watchword (Bibl.)

XXIII. 109-86-132-124-72-117-123-178. Uttered a harsh sound.

XXIV. 157-44-93-53-166-18-35-103. Forceful.

XXV. 156-154-74-169-70-57. To stop the flow.

WORDS

I. _____

II. _____

III. _____

IV. _____

V. _____

VI. _____

VII. _____

VIII. _____

IX _____

X. _____

XI. _____

XII. _____

XIII. _____

XIV. _____

XV. _____

XVI. _____

XVII. _____

XVIII. _____

XIX. _____

XX. _____

XXI. _____

XXII. _____

XXIII. _____

XXIV. _____

XXV. _____

NOTICE

This is the first of a series of ingenious literary puzzles invented by Elizabeth S. Kingsley for *The Saturday Review*. A new puzzle will be published each week, and the answer to the previous puzzle will appear regularly in this space. Let us know if the DIRECTIONS are clear. And after you have solved several of the puzzles we should like to know whether you think them too hard or too easy—our DEFINITIONS will be governed accordingly! Write to THE PUZZLE EDITOR, THE SATURDAY REVIEW, 25 WEST 45TH STREET, NEW YORK CITY.

As with many puzzle editors, Mrs. Kingsley felt that the feedback she got from a largely anonymous public was an important aspect of her job. While most of her mail was positive, on one occasion her faithful followers lambasted her for what they termed to be poor judgment. Her use of the word *tow-row* (meaning uproar or rumpus) unleashed a rash of letters criticizing her for using a slang expression in such a literary puzzle. One fan came to her rescue by pointing out that a passage in *Kidnapped* contained the expression "a tow-row of thunder." Obviously, if Robert Louis Stevenson thought it acceptable Mrs. Kingsley should be exonerated!

Sam Loyd, Lewis Carroll, Margaret Farrar, Torquemada and Elizabeth Kingsley are among the first-rate puzzlers of all time. Though they used diverse puzzles to amuse and stimulate their particular audiences, they shared a common bond in the love of creating original products.

The first double-crostic, as it appeared in *The Saturday Review of Literature* on March 31, 1934. (*See* Picture Answers, 17.)

A PANOPLY OF PUZZLES PRESENT

In centuries gone by, puzzling was an elitist, intellectual pursuit and had to compete for its devotees against literature, art and music. However, as literacy spread, social conditions changed and more and more people were able to engage in leisure-time activities; a spate of new entertainments and hobbies sprung up to occupy people's spare time. Today puzzles and other word games are pitted against a formidable array of opponents for their share of the leisure-time market. Television, backgammon, chess, bridge and other card games, pottery and macrame are just a few of their rivals. While these activities were either unknown or out of the reach of the masses years ago, their proponents have vigorously campaigned for and have now attracted hordes of faithful followers. Puzzles, however, have not only survived the increased competition, but are still a favorite pastime for millions of people.

How has a product which dates back to the origins of mankind managed to remain popular? The answer is simple. As people's needs changed so did puzzles. They have never been allowed to stagnate. Their physical appearance was altered; the clues were modernized; and new puzzle forms were constantly being invented. Puzzles today are very different than those of the eighteenth and nineteenth centuries. People no longer spend their evenings working charades, enigmas or logogriphs, and clues are no longer written in verse. In fact, most of today's puzzles presented in diagrams or grids are variations of the crossword, a twentieth-century invention. But no matter how different things are today, the basic aim of puzzling remains the same: to challenge one's ingenuity in a clever way.

A puzzler's motivation for seeking out a particular type of puzzle is multidimensional, for a puzzle may satisfy a wide range of needs and wants. Some puzzles are done for prestige: some people (especially Americans!) feel that to complete the London *Times* puzzles enhances one's intellectual status! Other puzzles are time fillers: a crossword can easily be completed while commuting or sitting in a doctor's waiting room. Still others are time killers: word searches require the ability simply to plow through a "field" of letters and search out

112

words—no mental taxation here at all! For certain people puzzles are well-formed habits; doing a specific puzzle every day at the same time helps keep them on an even keel. The reasons are multifarious, but there is one thing that all puzzle people have in common—their passion for puzzling!

Here is a small, but representative sampling of the wide range of puzzles available to the modern puzzler. The answers can be found in the "Picture Answers" section at the back of the book.

Puzzle 1

Each set of clues has a five-letter answer word in common, one that follows the first word and precedes the second word. The numbers indicate the points between which the answer should be placed.

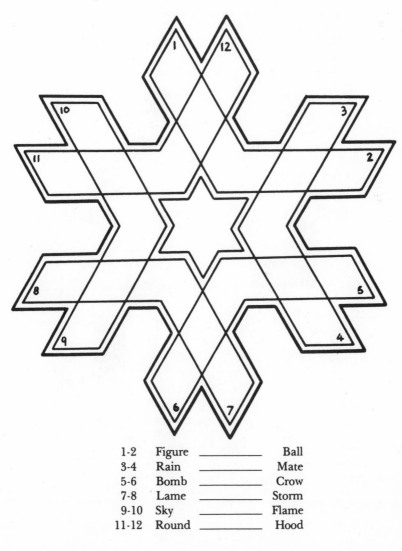

1-2	Figure	_____	Ball
3-4	Rain	_____	Mate
5-6	Bomb	_____	Crow
7-8	Lame	_____	Storm
9-10	Sky	_____	Flame
11-12	Round	_____	Hood

113

Puzzle 2

This is a crossword to literally flip over! The left side of the diagram is filled in and then the page is turned over so that the other half can be solved. Center words which read both ways form the connecting links.

ACROSS

1 Precedes coal and woman
5 Restful vacation spot
8 Topnotch: hyph. wd.
9 Sea eagle
10 Ornamental band
12 _____ of David
13 Nothing
14 Biblical pronoun
15 Heroic champion
17 Mother of Jupiter
19 Distance moved to the side: 2 wds.
20 Armbone
22 Traffic supervisor
23 Carpenter's need
25 Type of moth

DOWN

1 City transportation
2 Tomfoolery
3 College course: abbr.
4 Summarization
5 Salt: Fr.
6 Before birth
7 Cures
11 Time periods
14 New
16 _____ of mutton
18 Cut quickly
21 Pacino and Capone
24 Square yard: abbr.

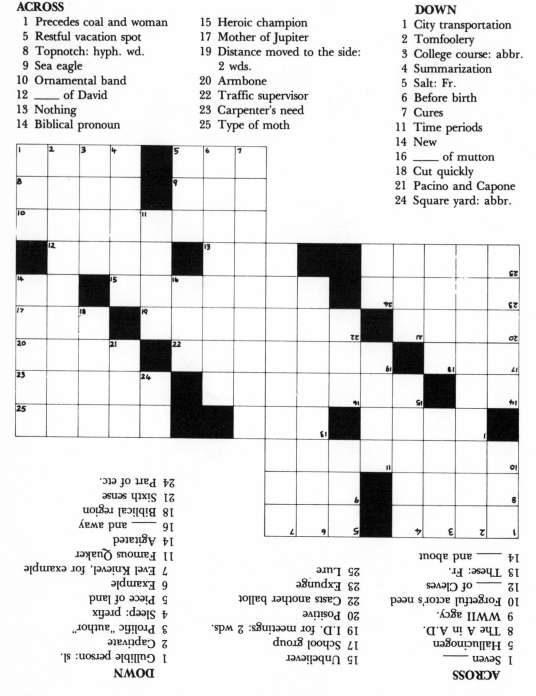

14 _____ and about
13 These: Fr.
12 _____ of Cleves
10 Forgetful actor's need
9 WWII agcy.
8 The A in A.D.
5 Hallucinogen
1 Seven _____

ACROSS

15 Unbeliever
17 School group
19 I.D. for meetings: 2 wds.
20 Positive
22 Casts another ballot
23 Expunge
25 Lure

DOWN

1 Gullible person: sl.
2 Captivate
3 Prolific "author"
4 Sleep: prefix
5 Piece of land
6 Example
7 Evel Knievel, for example
11 Famous Quaker
14 Agitated
16 _____ and away
18 Biblical region
21 Sixth sense
24 Part of etc.

114

Puzzle 3   This puzzle presents the answers which then must be placed in the grid to form an interlocking crossword.

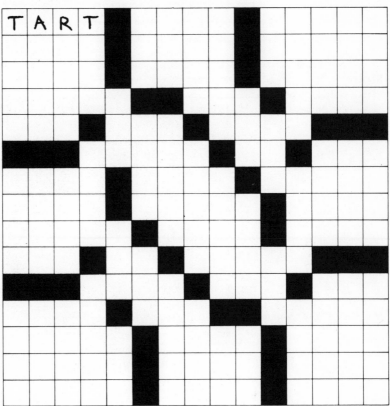

2 Letters	Sot	Oral	5 Letters	Swine
Be	Tat	Over	Aloud	Tango
We		Peer	Arena	Tenet
	4 Letters	Rake	Award	Titan
3 Letters	Acre	Reek	Aware	Waive
Act	Aide	Roan	Canoe	
Ass	Aloe	Scow	Crank	
Bay	Alto	Shot	Dowel	
Ear	Ante	Slat	Elate	
Ego	Camp	Soda	Gusty	
Eke	Clam	Spit	Later	
Ell	Dent	Stop	Limit	
Hie	Else	Stow	Merge	
Ilk	Erse	Tart	Orate	
Lie	Ewer	Tell	Piece	
Men	Game	Tent	Plane	
Oat	Hear	Term	Rouse	
Ode	Hide	Tire	Sense	
Owe	Idea	Toga	Shale	
Pro	Land	Vane	Slake	
Sap	Late	Vent	Slate	
Say	Noun	Year	Sleek	
Shy	Omen	Yoke		

Puzzle 4

Diagramless puzzles eliminate the black squares that denote word endings. The grid has to be numbered and filled in with black spaces to form a symmetrical diagram.

ACROSS
1 Derby or homburg
4 Desert horse
8 Sheltered side
10 Risks
12 It's O.K.
14 Cowrie and conch
16 ___ rates
18 River in N. England
20 Quiver
22 Brine
24 Rejuvenate
26 River mouth deposit
29 Act of courage
31 Disposition
32 ___ grease
34 Short treatise
37 Sailors
39 Kind of dancing
41 Enclosure
43 Covers
44 What the Supreme Court did
46 Dispatch
47 Repent
49 Stalemate
50 Coat of gold
51 Heavyweights
52 Sea eagle
53 Kind of mate
54 Yacht heading
55 Junior
57 Attract
58 Mistake
62 AM or FM
64 Mine entrance
66 4 gills
67 Platinum or nickel
69 Parking timer
72 Aeons
74 Corrected proof
77 Cypress
79 Renovate
81 Black birds
85 Under no conditions
86 Turning point
87 Nevada city
88 Songstress Horne
89 Tooth puller: abbr.

DOWN
1 Latch
2 Apportion
3 Harass
4 Paid notices
5 Cheer
6 You ___ always in my heart . . .
7 Waist cincher
9 Go inside
11 Eskimo vehicle
13 With leg or keeper
15 Sow
17 Libraries
19 Apparently true
21 Lively dances
23 Story line
25 Spider's trap
27 High craggy hill
28 Political activist org.
30 Period
33 Devastate
35 Milk top
36 Camper's shelter
37 Cookie keepers
38 Fruit drink
40 Couples
42 Dutch commune
43 Hermit
45 Caruso
46 Cabbage salad
47 Munched
48 Kind of poem
50 "Princess and the ___"
53 Race horse
56 Fabric pile
57 One who 47 down
59 Aries
60 Way: suffix
61 Ceremony
63 Dusky
65 Piece of canvas
68 Den
70 Level
71 Mississippi
73 With cold or bean
75 How a penny is earned
76 Improve
78 Nasty
80 Professionals, for short
82 Halloween
83 Reverse of
84 Station: abbr.

In this crossword one or more letters can fill a space. The numbers in parentheses indicate word lengths.

ACROSS

1 Embrace (5)
4 Detergent (4)
7 Arrests (5)
10 Tropical shrub (4)
11 Melancholy (4)
12 Corroded (3)
13 Mealtime prayer (5)
14 Based on observation (9)
16 Sailor (3)
18 Harbor fixture (4)
19 Sonorously (9)
21 Water tower (9)
25 Endeavor (6)
26 High note: 2 wds. (3)
27 Gleaming (8)
30 Strips (8)
32 Gaelic (4)
33 Mutineer (5)
34 Inborn quality (10)
38 Peculiar (3)
41 Scandinavians (5)
42 Anglo-Saxon slave (4)
43 Read carefully (6)
44 Garden tools (4)
45 Farm animals (4)
46 Ooze (4)

DOWN

1 Adhere to (5)
2 Taj Mahal site (4)
3 Ultramodern movement: 2 wds. (11)
4 Seriously (7)
5 Astringent (4)
6 Most energetic (8)
7 Hollywood bigwig (4)
8 Pertaining to the eye (5)
9 Fine fur (4)
15 Asian land (4)
17 Tiny tunneler (3)
19 View (5)
20 Sailing vessel (4)
22 Grows (9)
23 Stack (4)
24 Pod vegetables (4)
28 Repeat (7)
29 Brevity (9)
30 Forces down (9)
31 Chest bone (3)
34 Western state (5)
35 Compass point (3)
36 Promontory (4)
37 Sufficient: poet. (4)
39 Syrian tribesman (5)
40 Profound (4)

British puzzles are predominately of the cryptic clue variety. For those unfamiliar with cryptic clues, definition type clues are also available. (Reprinted by permission of *The Puzzler*.)

STRAIGHT
CLUES

ACROSS

1 Big pancake
5 Sour
9 Bellicose
11 Part of an 'I', e.g.
12 Requirements
14 Digit
16 Make a mistake
17 Magnitude
19 Dandy
21 Sign of fatigue
23 Light banter
25 Farm birds
26 Remaining
28 A colour
29 Row
30 Copy
32 Outgoing tide
34 To empty
37 Wet (of weather)
38 Laugh secretly
39 Eve's garden
40 Fieldsman

DOWN

1 Hen, e.g.
2 Archer's ammunition
3 Enlist in
4 Shout approval
6 Variety of 28A
7 Disagreed
8 Stupid person
10 Retain
13 Arid
15 Bid
17 Scandinavian
18 Unpunished
20 Preposition
22 Long time
24 Beer seller
27 Pitchy substance
28 Part of harness
31 Floury substance
33 Rope loop
34 Re-colour
35 Notch
36 Hold enthralled

CRYPTIC
CLUES

ACROSS

1 Panic, sailor? — only when out of the frying-pan . . . (8)
5 Sharp for an anti-crime organisation (4)
9 Not exactly exhibiting pacifist tendencies (7)
11 Fires back and is part of one's character, perhaps (5)
12 Requires more than one 39A to be redesigned (5)
14 Company as opposed to a crowd in numerical terms (3)
16 Wander in serried ranks (3)
17 Glue in bulk (4)
19 He might look vainglorious (3)
21 Open wide as a chasm (4)
23 Banter (huskily!) (5)
25 They get fat in December (5)
26 Socialist over . . . (4)

28 . . . Communist shade (3)
29 Knotter? (4)
30 Mimic one of one's ancestors (3)
32 Go back down the beach (3)
34 Exhaust in cold rainy weather (5)
37 Such a season is bad for cricket (5)
38 Laugh in one's sleeve (7)
39 Badly need a garden (4)
40 Last in the field is he? (8)

DOWN

1 Horrible sounding bird (4)
2 A standard of straightness — when on target? (5)
3 Josephine at home after a break (4)
4 A hundred here milling about for food and drink (5)
6 Red automobile belongs to me, it seems (7)
7 Disagreed — by agreement? (8)

118

8 Singularly stupid law on occasion (3)
10 Retain part of the castle (4)
13 Not 37A—how boring (3)
15 Proposal from 20D with hesitation (5)
17 Scandinavian stew ingredient? (5)
18 He is at liberty north of the border (8)
20 A preposition which is no longer good (3)
22 The senile show theirs for a long time (3)

24 Fishy vendor of beer (7)
27 Jack's art form (3)
28 One of two with a bit on the end (4)
31 Papa's table offers macaroni, ravioli, etc. (5)
33 Sounds like something to eat in a shallow bay (5)
34 Colour in its third year (3)
35 Arrest the devil before it's too late (4)
36 To get one such is to gain control (4)

Puzzle 7   This British-style diagram (with American type clues) is a two-fer. Each ACROSS and DOWN number consists of two clues which must be placed in one or the other diagram.

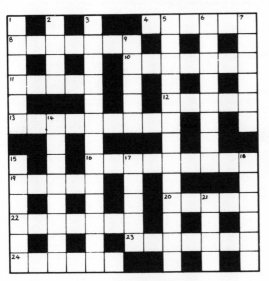

ACROSS

4 Mount; handwriting
8 Plant; shoal
10 Forming a ring; narrative
11 Mistake; creamy white
12 Russian mountains; approaches
13 Peerless; apart
16 In plain sight; dull persons
19 Reasoning method; the Gem State
20 Impatient; likeness
22 Weaving device; small ears of corn
23 Nomadic; snarled
24 Unrefined; dismal

DOWN

1 Allot; bids
2 Cicatrix; gambling game
3 Devastate: 3 wds.; trial stenographer: 2 wds.
5 Baseball player: 2 wds.; conferences
6 Tries to equal; unlucky: hyph. wd.
7 Forceful push; abhor
9 Forgo; racing vessel
14 Delight; fellow next door
15 Booed and ____; dive
17 Command; faith
18 Surrenders; Gallic gestures
21 Confederate; firm hold

Puzzle 8

Black squares are eliminated in this continuous form puzzle. The heavy lines indicate word delineations. Each ACROSS and DOWN clue is actually composed of several clues, one for each word in that particular row of squares. (Reprinted by permission of *The Puzzler*.)

ACROSS

1 Furnish; rower's blade; plausible; newt
2 Clergyman's title; ridicule; negative
3 Assessed too highly; caused to limp; born
4 Change; inconsistent; convince
5 An oval; a tear in flesh
6 Private combat; share out; copied
7 Bargain; infrequent; liquid measure; stage play
8 Atone for; agreement; yearly
9 E. European; dual; Japanese sash; land measure
10 Joint; 'Hamlet' character; song of praise
11 Bellow; hard to catch; withdraw
12 Dismay; go ahead; more mature
13 Flaky rock; insinuation; run with long easy strides
14 Wheel's toothlike projection; complete; flippancy; dishonourable
15 Coming to nothing; crop up; small Turkish coin
16 Stay around; make more fertile; units of power
17 Assert; before; flower; optical fringe?

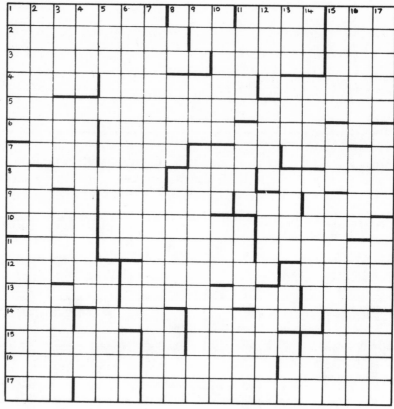

DOWN

1 Demonstrated; office table; rogues
2 Re-establish worth of; irrational fear of foreigners
3 Finished; spring; gather in; torment
4 Extremely; intolerant; sudden desire
5 Unable to be mended; missive
6 Expensive; of space; deep hole; anger
7 Businessman; at no time
8 Poem; bitter-juiced plant; clergyman; U.S. divorce city
9 Say further; sailor; personal details
10 Widow; very cold; Adam's wife; promoting fear
11 Elegance of movement; preposition; observed; depravity

12 Peru's capital; roster; poet or singer; attractive
13 Carp's relative; cement constituent; digit; decay; female sheep
14 Place to sleep; heavenly body; smartly (dressed); buddy
15 Boredom; Hautes-Pyrenees river; small sausage
16 Enemy; mass of fish eggs; female horse; statements of facts
17 Obsolete Manx territorial division; valley; simple; perform ablutions

Puzzle 9   This mixed-up puzzle has answers that read backwards and upwards. BACK clues must be filled in from right to left and UP clues, from bottom to top.

BACK

1 Cushions
2 River ____
3 Window ledge
4 Baking chamber
5 Work unit
6 Silkworm
7 Story
8 ____ Galahad
10 Donated
11 Confederates
13 Rubbed out
17 City official
20 Circle part
21 Malt brew
22 Military student
23 Pedal digits
24 New flower
25 Simple
26 Scatter
29 Scarlet
30 ____ and then
33 Chemistry vial: 2 wds.
35 Tune
37 Entertained
39 Steel source
40 Lamprey
41 Routine
42 Ore deposit
43 Dark bread
44 Sharpen
45 Slipped
49 For each
52 Cole ____

UP

9 Choler
11 Upon
12 Molten rock
14 Hindu robe
15 Wicked

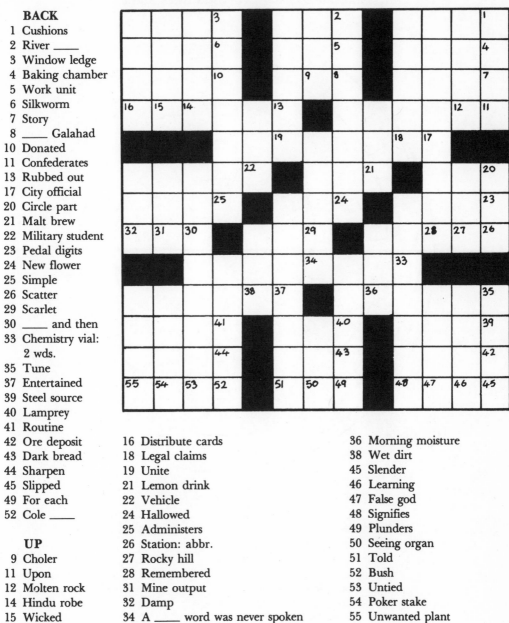

16 Distribute cards
18 Legal claims
19 Unite
21 Lemon drink
22 Vehicle
24 Hallowed
25 Administers
26 Station: abbr.
27 Rocky hill
28 Remembered
31 Mine output
32 Damp
34 A ____ word was never spoken

36 Morning moisture
38 Wet dirt
45 Slender
46 Learning
47 False god
48 Signifies
49 Plunders
50 Seeing organ
51 Told
52 Bush
53 Untied
54 Poker stake
55 Unwanted plant

Puzzle 10

This puzzle requires an ability to think in circles. It can be worked in an outward or inward-bound direction. The numbers indicate the lengths of the answer words.

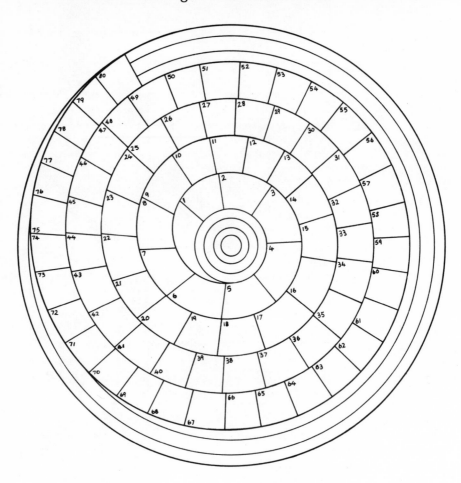

OUTWARD

1-4 Three feet
5-8 _____ Ferber
9-12 Knight, to a lady in distress
13-16 Jester
17-25 Nonsense words
26-31 Noted French writer
32-38 Movie "bad guy"
39-44 White-plumed herons
45-50 Loudly lament
51-57 Foodfish of the Atlantic
58-63 Pranks
64-67 Sandwich shop, for short
68-73 Besiege
74-80 Girl's salutation

INWARD

80-78 By all means
77-73 Highway vehicle
72-66 Marsh plant
65-63 Sullivan and McMahon
62-57 Fill suitcase again
56-54 _____-liver oil
53-48 Perennial flower
47-41 Noah or Daniel _____
40-35 Cheerful and friendly
34-30 Organ of the body
29-25 Garbage
24-22 Title of respect
21-19 Flow back
18-14 Northern Alaska home
13-4 With a certain tennis stroke
3-1 Sunbeam

Puzzle 11

In this honeycomb puzzle each answer is a six-letter word and will circle its number in either a clockwise or counterclockwise direction.

1 & or ¢
2 "Old Faithful"
3 Area
4 Meet and discuss
5 Betrothed
6 ____ juice
7 An alloy
8 Prague residents
9 Plan
10 Come out of
11 Promise
12 Drinking glass

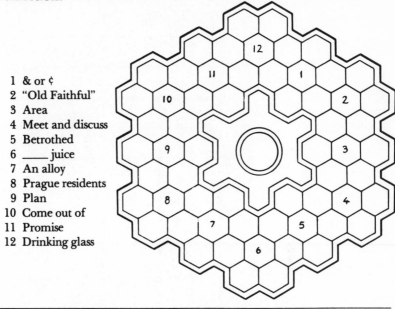

Puzzle 12

In this petalled puzzle the answers read in a curve from the number on the outside to the center of the flower. Each number starts two five-letter words; one goes in a clockwise direction and the other in a counterclockwise direction.

CLOCKWISE

1 Article of dinnerware
2 Singer ____ John
3 Penalties
4 Type of farm
5 Nice weather forecast
6 Helpers
7 Goes with draw and face
8 No-no
9 Montana city
10 Prices
11 Thought about
12 Cheerfully
13 ____ paper
14 Ms. Baker or Ms. Keaton
15 Palm off
16 Back of a bound book
17 Speak eloquently
18 Famous battle

COUNTERCLOCKWISE

1 Factory
2 Make happy
3 Beau of earlier days
4 Duplicate
5 Watercraft
6 Being from outer space
7 Wharves
8 Now
9 Senator from Tennessee
10 Ice ____
11 Engine
12 Keen enjoyment
13 Hindu social class
14 Uses a towel
15 Pasture
16 Sudsy
17 Think
18 Come into existence

123

Puzzle 13

The answers to these definitions wind their way around the diagram. Some words even overlap. Because answers may be written from right to left or up and down number sequences must be followed.

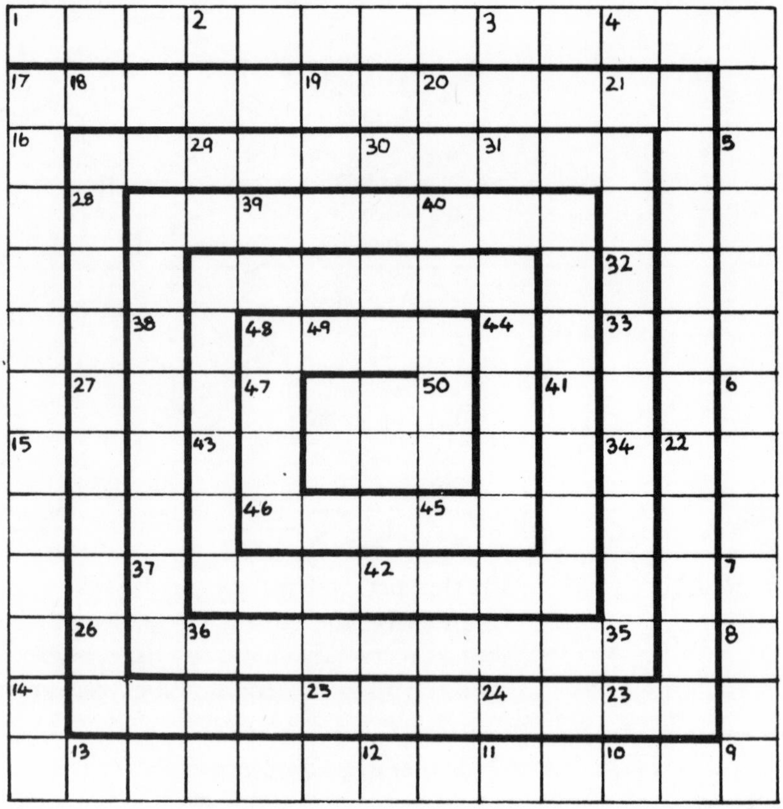

Grid numbers (as positioned in the diagram):
Row 1: 1, 2, 3, 4
Row 2: 17, 18, 19, 20, 21
Row 3: 16, 29, 30, 31, 5
Row 4: 28, 39, 40
Row 5: 32
Row 6: 38, 48, 49, 44, 33
Row 7: 27, 47, 50, 41, 6
Row 8: 15, 43, 34, 22
Row 9: 46, 45
Row 10: 37, 42, 7
Row 11: 26, 36, 35, 8
Row 12: 14, 25, 24, 23
Row 13: 13, 12, 11, 10, 9

1 Outdo
2 Persuasive
3 Start
4 Triple rhyme
5 Distinctive group of people
6 More frozen
7 God of Love
8 Girl's name
9 Ditto
10 Native of ancient Media
11 Transferable design
12 Bone-building element
13 Reddish brown
14 One-time capital of Germany
15 Investigation
16 Grain
17 Affirmative
18 Catching sight of
19 Nut
20 French society
21 Wickedness

22 Tropical storm
23 Without repetition
24 Fragrant wood
25 Attainment
26 Liquor
27 Evergreen
28 Deadly mob action
29 Group of singers
30 Plunge into
31 Outcry
32 Increase
33 Retain
34 Memorable time
35 Paid driver
36 Prod
37 ____ Washington
38 Talent
39 Customary
40 First king of Portugal
41 Sisterhood
42 Infectious fever

43 Hangup
44 Refuge
45 Vowel mark
46 Sedan, for one
47 Pull by a rope
48 Be indebted
49 Renege
50 Two-wheeled carriage

124

Puzzle 14

In this partially completed puzzle the consonants have already been filled in. Vowels only must be placed in the grid.

L			F	■		B		T	■	B	R		S	S
	X	L		■	S		R		■			S		L
S	T		W		L		N	X		S	P		N	
S			■	S		■	S		L	T	■		D	D
	L	D	H		N	D	■	S		M		■	■	■
■				N	G		R	■	P		Y		F	F
D		F	T	■		B		T		N		V		R
	C		■		S		P		D	■			R	
S	H		R	■	R		N				N	N		■
H		L	D		P	■	L		G		L	■	■	
■				N		S		S	T	R		T	C	H
M		P	■		T	C	H	■		T	■	R		
	C			N		R			R		G		L	
T	R			T			R					D		R
H		L	L		■	W		R	D	■	T		N	T

Puzzle 15

In a Knight's Tour puzzle a short saying can be deciphered by moving from one letter to another in the same manner that a knight moves on a chessboard (e.g., one square either horizontally or vertically and one square diagonally.) Start at the heart.

♡	T	A	W	V	T	L	H
B	T	I	I	D	I	H	K
G	I	E	E	O	O	T	U
P	R	H	L	D	O	N	S
T	I	E	S	L	A	H	D
R	A	L	L	N	R	I	R
C	W	T	A	T	A	N	T
R	E	U	O	A	E	A	T

The answers to this puzzle are broken down into their component syllables and arranged alphabetically in the box at the top. The numbers in parentheses indicate the syllable length of each answer. Every syllable will be used. When completed, the first and last letters, reading down, spell out an epigram preceded by its author.

A AN AT ATE AU AV BAN BANE BER CON CRAT CU DI DO EL EN
FLA GO HER I I IR ISH KI KI LAM LATE LES LOUS ME MEZ MIN
MIN NEWS NINE NISM O OB PROOF RA REEL RICE RISH RUS STIP
STRAT STRUCT SU TA TA TACH TAG TER TIC TIONS TLER TO U
U UM UR US WA YA ZA

---

1. A pink, long-necked, wading bird (3) F L A M I N G O
2. A cattle or horse thief (2) __ __ __ __ __ __ __
3. An arrogant, dictatorial person (3) __ __ __ __ __ __ __ __
4. Exile (2) __ __ __ __ __ __
5. A freestone peach (3) __ __ __ __ __ __ __
6. Lyrical book of the Old Testament (4) __ __ __ __ __ __ __ __ __ __ __ __
7. Make fast to something; affix (2) __ __ __ __ __ __
8. Direct light upon; illuminate (4) __ __ __ __ __ __ __ __ __
9. Spell out the terms of an agreement (3) __ __ __ __ __ __ __ __ __
10. Low-lying, layered clouds (2) __ __ __ __ __ __ __
11. Block or retard the way of; clog (2) __ __ __ __ __ __ __ __
12. Front of theater balcony (3) __ __ __ __ __ __ __ __
13. Suave (2) __ __ __ __ __ __
14. Individually-owned apartment (5) __ __ __ __ __ __ __ __ __ __ __
15. Mythological strong man (3) __ __ __ __ __ __ __ __
16. ____ Sea, stew, setter, or potato (2) __ __ __ __ __
17. A Japanese dish (4) __ __ __ __ __ __ __
18. Mutual opposition; hostility (4) __ __ __ __ __ __ __ __ __
19. Extremely precise about details (4) __ __ __ __ __ __ __ __ __
20. Greed (3) __ __ __ __ __ __ __
21. Short current events moving picture (2) __ __ __ __ __ __ __ __
22. Impervious to rain (3) __ __ __ __ __ __ __ __ __

Puzzle 17   These cryptograms use number instead of letter substitution. Each number represents one of the three letters shown with it on the telephone dial. A number does not necessarily represent the same letter each time.

1. 6269 2 626 47 668

   7873778484687 2322873 43

   844657 48 274647 223 5825.

2. 43 968 5665 5453 9687

   72777678 7468647274, 968 6333

   843 8747.

3. 843 626 946 844657 43 56697

   3837984464 259297 477482837

   84673 63 87 946 36.

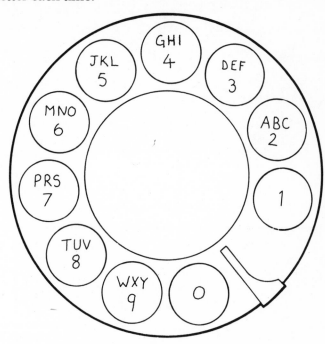

Puzzle 18   This puzzle is a variation on the anagram. Each line is worked as a unit. First solve definition 1, drop a letter and rearrange the rest to form definition 2, etc. The dropped letters go into the end boxes which, when completed and read vertically, spell out related words.

1 Dining boards
2 "Beauty
   and the _____"
3 Glut
4 Ventilating
5 Wood pattern
6 Sounded a bell
7 Raved
8 Barter
9 Palm fruit
10 Located
11 Graded
12 Challenge
13 Husky-voiced
14 Portion
15 Epochs
16 Cover girls
17 Rounded roofs
18 Any

19 Father or mother
20 Thin candle
21 Saucy

22 Sylvan demigods
23 Salvers
24 Asterisk

1	2	3	
4	5	6	
7	8	9	
10	11	12	
13	14	15	
16	17	18	
19	20	21	
22	23	24	

Puzzle 19   This type of puzzle requires no vocabulary skills; it's just a matter of placing the words into the correct spaces on the grid so that they all interlock.

3 Letters	4 Letters		Miler	Ostler
Bar	A.H.S.A.	Odds	Mount	Ox-rail
Dam	Aids	Over	Pinto	Retain
Ego	Airs	Pair	Studs	Rumble
Leg	Call	Poke	Throw	Shoo-in
Nag	Cast	Ring	Trace	Stumer
Nip	Done	Span	Train	Tandem
Par	Duga	Spur		
Run	Dust		6 Letters	7 Letters
Sod	Ears	5 Letters	Driver	Also-ran
Top	Ease	Alter	Exmoor	Fanfare
	Meet	Apron	Master	Infield
		Brush		

Paddock	**8 Letters**	Good hands	Plank fence	Snubbing post
Rat-tail	Tack room	Inner rein	Stem mother	Spear of honor
Records	Tapadero	Kirby gate		Thoroughbred
Take off		Outer hand	**12 Letters**	
Tow-ring	**9 Letters**		Becher's Brook	**16 Letters**
Unleash	About turn	**10 Letters**	Championship	Fine harness horse
	Bad actors	Dipped back	Dude wrangler	Naragansett pacer
	Enclosure	Opera board	Equestrienne	

Puzzle 20

This puzzle is merely a search for words through seemingly random letters. The words can read backwards, forwards, up, down or diagonally. Words often overlap and some letters may be used more than once.

```
R O V E R P L I C R O Q U E T H N G F R E N C L
H O P P O N E N T Y R E N R L W A O U H S U P B
O P L A Y I N G S I D E N O A E U N M C H G T A
M T U H N P L A R E I O F L L L A B D A E D T U
E O W L I S R L T Y N E U L A H J V M O L I K L
S H D N L E R F G N A C H B O L I A E R L L A K
T S W W K D H N A T R L A O L I K J Y P N M E S
A P D I L I S C H T Y I P C H E C K S P I N S T
K O R C R S U E R K H G N N A I T R H A G B J R
E T I K L E R U A A I M C H I Y R A D N U O B O
S S T E R O O E W H T Y O B A L L S P L I N E K
C U E T F C R T A K E O F F J N U Y S N M J U E
S P R F N B L A Y U P U O R G H D E U Q S I B S
D R I V E K A T S G N I N R U T U P R I G H T S
```

Aim	Court	In hand	Ordinary hit	Side spin
Approach	Croquet	In play	Peel	Split
Arch	Dead ball	Join up	Peg	Stop shot
Balls	Double tap	Lawn	Playing side	Striker
Baulk	Drive	Layup	Pull	Strokes
Bisque	Feather off	Leave	Push	Takeoff
Boundary	Flag	Line	Roll	Turning stake
Break	Foul	Make a hoop	Rover	Uprights
Cannon	Group	Mallet	Run a hoop	Wicket
Check spin	Home stake	Opponent	Rush	Wire

ON BEYOND PUZZLES

Board Games and Quiz Shows

One of the most distinguishing characteristics of puzzle solving is that it is essentially a solitary pursuit. Although you are engaged in a battle of wits with an unseen opponent, the puzzle constructor, essentially you are in competition with yourself. Will you enhance your self-esteem by completing the puzzle? Can you surpass your previous attempts? Is a particular puzzle series too easy, too difficult or just right for you? Do you want to attempt harder puzzles? Or do you actually prefer simpler puzzles? You can challenge yourself as much or as little as possible. There are no scores or judges; and only you can determine — and control — the extent of your involvement.

Antithetical to the traditional puzzler and his singularity are the board games and television quiz shows which are based on puzzle themes. Fast-paced, competitive and played with several people, these games and shows bear only a faint resemblance to the puzzles from which they descended. They usually involve a superimposed time element; the puzzle must be solved within a specified time. There is overt competition between opposing teams or players. Scores are kept, prizes may be awarded and the outcome is sometimes reported or broadcast to thousands, even millions of people. Quite a contrast to the image of a puzzler curled up by the fireplace with pencil in hand, totally absorbed in his hobby.

Traditional puzzlers can and do wince at the bastardization of their favorite pastime, but the enormous popularity of puzzle board games and TV quiz shows is yet another affirmation of the public's fascination with words. Eliza Doolittle may have been "sick of words," but almost everybody else is crazy about them!

Board Games

Scrabble was first introduced to the mass American market in the 1950s and immediately created a demand which the manufacturers, Selchow & Righter, have had difficulty filling ever since. Based on anagrams and crossword puzzles, this game allows two to four players to match wits by forming interlocking words with numbered letter tiles. The object is to amass as many points as possible by using the premium spaces on the board, triple-word and triple-letter spaces being the most valuable. If no time limit per turn is imposed, the game can literally last for hours. There are French, Spanish, German, Italian and Russian editions of the game and sales mount each year.

To meet the demand for a forum where interested Scrabble players could compete against each other Selchow & Righter sponsor Scrabble Players Clubs. These groups enable complete strangers to play against each other under semistandardized conditions. S & R conservatively estimates that there are approximately five thousand official members in the United States. Actually, the number of people involved in these clubs is probably much higher because not everyone is an "official" member.

Through these clubs, Scrabble players can amass expert points much in the same manner as tournament bridge players. As in other competitive games, a hierarchy of players has evolved. The experts are recognizable by their ability to play aggressively and accumulate very high scores (500 points is not atypical.) Their tactics involve using obscure words (anything goes, as long as it is contained in Funk and Wagnalls Standard College Dictionary), trying to land as many high-scoring letters on triple-letter and triple-word spaces as possible, preventing their opponents from using these same spaces, and saving their letters to form seven-letter words, or bingos, which are worth an additional fifty points.

Scrabble players clubs are found all across the country and are made up of people of all ages and occupations. In the course of an evening one plays three games of Scrabble with a time limit of three minutes per turn. The prevailing mood is sober; small talk and jokes are frowned upon. Players are there primarily to test their mental agility against each other and the atmosphere is very word conscious. Club sessions are held on a weekly or biweekly basis. A core of regulars attends every meeting, and newcomers are warmly welcomed (in between games). If you're an avid player a Scrabble players club is an optimal way of meeting like-minded people.

Periodically S & R will join forces with a local recreation organization or a players club and sponsor a Scrabble tournament. Playing rules are similar to those already mentioned but the mood is intensely competitive. Players who habitually win at Scrabble against their friends and relatives are dismayed to discover their shortcomings when pitted against the experts. These competitions run for several weeks and players are elim-

The New York City Department of Recreation sponsors an annual Scrabble tournament that attracts hundreds of contestants. Playing three games in a four-hour-period requires lots of stamina, but the most intrepid players thrive on intense competition.

The Scrabble Players tee shirt can be purchased from Selchow & Righter, but it's much more prestigious to win one at a tournament.

inated at each session until a champion emerges during the final playoffs. Prizes are nominal—Scrabble Players tee shirts, games and a savings bond for the grand winner. For the people who compete in these tournaments, the main attraction is not the prizes but the opportunity to test themselves against other players on their level. One denizen of the club-tournament milieu, Roz Grossman, summed up her reasons for competing in the following poem:

132

COME SCRABBLE WITH ME AND BE MY LOVE

I hate to play Scrabble
With people who babble
My psyche gets balky
When they become talky.

I hate to play Scrabble
With people who dabble
In encyclopedias
I think they are tedious.

I hate to play Scrabble
With people who gabble
Of xebecs and xysters
I think they are shysters.

I hate to play Scrabble
With people who wabble
All over the board
Until they have scored.

But I LOVE to play Scrabble
With my kind of rabble
We're not erudite but
We keep our mouth quite shut.

Among us there's nary
A new dictionary
We keep the game moving—
HELL, WHAT ARE WE PROVING?

A faster-paced version of Scrabble is played with Scrabble Crossword Cubes where fourteen lettered cubes are placed in a container and thrown out on a table. An egg timer is used, and each player has exactly two minutes to form a mini-crossword puzzle. The object is to gain as many points as possible using all the cubes. Any number of people can play and the game ends when a previously agreed-upon score is reached by one player. Another variation of this game uses word cubes instead of letter cubes, the object being to form sentences in crossword fashion. As the possibilities for composing ridiculous sentences run very high, this game tends to be more light-hearted than other Scrabble variations.

Scrabble Scoring Anagrams is equally action oriented. Players simultaneously try to form words using a core of exposed letter tiles. Once a player has formed a word, any other player can capture it by adding one or more letters and rearranging the original word. In this manner TAKE can become STEAK. Players with the ability to transpose letters, think quickly and compete briskly find this a stimulating game.

R.S.V.P. adds an extra dimension to word games. One person competes against another by forming interlocking words on his side of the grid while impeding his opponent's ability to form words on the other side. Basically the game is an extension of Scrabble; the added novelty is working both sides of a grid.

Jumble, "that scrambled word game," is a derivation of a widely syndicated newspaper column of the same name. Letter combinations such as YARIN must be unscrambled to form RAINY and placed in a grid such as this,

where one or more letters are circled. The circled letters are then placed in another grid and rearranged to form an answer which is suggested by an accompanying cartoon. Jumble challenges one's ability to extract ordinary words from juxtaposed letters.

Other board games offer players similar opportunities to measure their abilities against another's adeptness. There is always some element of luck involved in these games, for you can stimulate your mind only to the extent of the letters in your hand. An added bonus for regular players is the development of a specialized vocabulary peculiar to word games. BEY, DARB and AI may not be the most commonly uttered words in your speaking repertoire, but their use at a crucial point in a word game can turn the score around in your favor.

Additional attempts at making puzzle solving a group experience instead of a solitary activity include the development of oversized puzzle grids, sometimes six-feet long. These puzzles are especially fun at parties as ice-breakers to get things moving. There are oversized crossword puzzles, word searches and

Six feet of crossword clues can satisfy a lot of puzzle addicts at once!

even jigsaw crosswords, where the puzzle comes unassembled and the pieces must be put back together—probably the only crossword you can solve without a pencil!

The plethora of puzzle-oriented games on the market attests to their popularity. While nothing can surpass the involvement of a puzzler in solving a challenging puzzle alone, multiplayer word games do provide entertaining diversions.

On the Air

Wow, GEE, REALLY, SUPER, GREAT, A-OKAY, UGH, OH NO, ARGHH are words frequently shrieked by contestants in the land of the television game show. And if these expressions aren't readily on the tip of one's tongue, there's always jumping, clapping, somersaulting or doing headstands to express one's emotions. The insulated world of the paper-and-pencil puzzlist doesn't exist amid the TV sets, cameras, audiences, blaring lights, horns, gadgetry, puzzle boards and general cacophony at game show tapings. Perhaps only puzzlers born under the sign of Gemini can coexist in the voiceless world of traditional puzzling and the boisterousness of quiz shows. Puzzle purists might regard game shows as a malignment of their craft but they are legitimate derivatives of word puzzles.

"Concentration" is a long-running American television show which uses a rebus as its game board. Two contestants vie against each other for lucrative prizes by "concentrating" on a game board sectioned into thirty numbered cubes with prizes

The "Concentration" rebus is always deciphered for the TV audience.

"Ah, sweet mystery of life," a perfect motto for "Concentration" contestants.

written on the reverse side. When it is his turn, the player calls out two numbers, with the object of trying to match up the prizes on the reverse side. When a match is made, the two corresponding pieces of the rebus are revealed. The rebus might be a familiar quotation, a famous person or place or something currently in vogue. The first contestant to decipher the rebus has an opportunity for the grand prize, which involves reading a fully revealed rebus in ten seconds. There's a high premium

on speed, something not found in ordinary puzzling. Nor are the substantial prizes!

"Cross-Wits" is a recent newcomer to evening game show audiences in America. Two teams vie against each other by solving a crossword puzzle in which all the clues and answers relate to a topic which could be a person, place or thing. Thus, after solving the puzzle the team must go one step further by putting all the clues together and uncoding the theme of the puzzle. The grid is merely a skeletal crossword with about eight to ten clues, such as this one in which "comedians" was the theme:

It's not easy to fill in a crossword grid with the clock ticking away, but the monetary prizes provide a strong incentive for speeding up one's thinking.

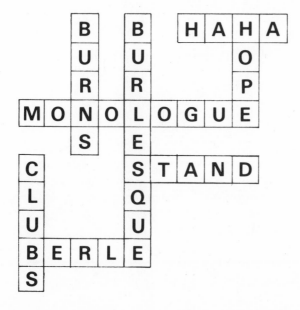

Clues in this game tend to be humorous: HA HA, for example, was defined as "follows mini." Again the emphasis is on speed and little intellectual skill is required. The audience commiserates or rejoices with the teams, and the overall atmosphere is frolicsome.

These puzzle shows attract eager contestants, paying sponsors and loyal viewers. Their appeal may lie in the vicarious pleasure home viewers get by watching an ordinary person win something for nothing or by answering questions which stump the contestants. Game show participants may not be "true" puzzlers, those whose love of word games goad them on to ever more difficult testing of their intellectual prowess, but nonetheless puzzle game shows are a logical extension of our civilization—a combination of twentieth-century technology with an age-old, ever-popular pastime.

So widespread is the appeal of puzzles that they have often been found in the most unexpected places. In the art world, Steve Gianakos, a young painter, recently exhibited a series of puzzle-inspired canvases that are full of humor, one of which is pictured below.

Crosswords appearing in places other than their normal habitat appeal to the public's thirst for unusual novelties. Recognizing this, *The New York Times* has produced tee shirts and tote bags with its famous puzzle printed on them. Available from other manufacturers are tee shirts sporting a "Concentration"-type rebus, panties for girls with a pictorial crossword design, and crossword toilet paper. Previous gimmicks, no longer on the market, included plastic-covered crossword

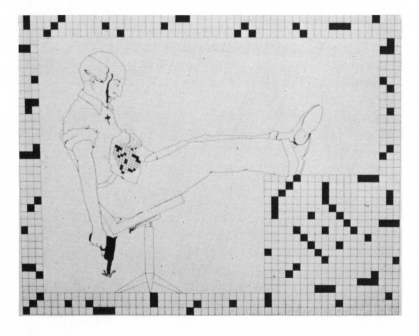

A crossword canvas by Steve Gianakos. This crossword suicide might have been avoided had the fellow owned a good crossword dictionary.

What will they think of next?

Of all the ways to say "Happy Birthday," a rebus card is one of the nicest.

placemats, rebus plates and bowls, and needlepoint crossword puzzles. Publishers of greeting cards, ever on the alert for unusual ideas, have used rebuses and word games on birthday and get well messages. These items may or may not have had a long life, but the mere fact that they were—and still are!— produced says something about the ever-present lure of puzzles.

PUZZLE LEAGUES

Like other hobbyists, puzzlers have formed associations to institutionalize their pastime, groups where they can meet people with similar interests and perpetuate the art of puzzling. In the United States two puzzle groups are especially noteworthy because of the quality of puzzles produced for their respective publications and the camaraderie between their members. These are the National Puzzlers' League (NPL) and the American Cryptogram Association (ACA), both nonprofit recreational organizations formed by and for puzzlers wishing to promote specific types of puzzles unavailable elsewhere. Although the ACA is a spin-off of the NPL with some overlap of membership, basically the two groups are oriented toward different kinds of people.

The NPL, originally called the Eastern Puzzlers' League (EPL), was launched by thirty-four puzzlers on July 4, 1883. The all-male enclave gathered at Pythagoras Hall in New York City to hold the first of its many conventions. These were elite puzzlers, composers of highly erudite works who had become aware of one another's interests through the puzzle columns, departments and periodicals that flourished in the last quarter of the nineteenth century. The original membership was restricted to men living east of the Mississippi. There were two conventions a year and members were entitled to receive the league's magazine, *The Eastern Enigma*, which surprisingly did not contain any puzzles. Rather, it concerned itself with members' verses, skits and somewhat technical articles on obsolete words and reference works, puzzle construction and puzzle history. The tone and content were exceedingly scholarly, befitting the elite audience that had come together to revel in the mystique of their craft. Typical of the essays published during this initial period were: "Digging for Diamonds," a treatise on form puzzles in the shape of a diamond; "On the Square," a historical piece about word square derivations; and "Olden Puzzledom," a recapitulation of puzzle development in magazines from 1865 to 1875. *The Eastern Enigma* was issued sporadically, depending on the whim of the editors and the number of contributions available. Editors were selected at each convention and served until the subsequent convention at which time they chose to renew or discontinue their tenure. Thus, the earliest years of the EPL's existence were primarily devoted to maintaining the status of puzzling as a highly cerebral activity confined to an elite core of intellectuals.

Changes were gradually introduced, but the essence of the organization remained the same: "to provide a pastime of mental relaxation for lovers of word puzzles, to raise the standard of puzzling to a higher intellectual level, and to establish and foster friendships among its widely scattered members."

In 1920 the EPL changed its name to the National Puzzlers' League to reflect the removal of the geographical restrictions. Current membership is approximately 250, with a majority of people still residing east of the Mississippi. However, practically every one of the United States is represented as well as Europe, Australia and Africa.

Since women have traditionally been avid puzzlers, it was impossible to maintain the all-male composition of the league. Women were admitted without fanfare in 1910, primarily because the spouses and sisters of members had surreptitiously infiltrated the NPL. The widespread use of noms-de-plume by the members made it easy to camouflage one's identity behind a nonsexist nom. The most famous infiltrator was "Rhayle Rhoader," whose femaleness long escaped the notice of the puzzlers with whom she corresponded. The respect she earned for her puzzles paved the way for other women being welcomed into the specialized league.

The name change, removal of residency requirements and inclusion of women were all minor changes compared to the facelift that *The Eastern Enigma* underwent. First, the name was shortened to *The Enigma*. Next, a puzzle department, Penetralia, was introduced in 1900. In 1910 it became a permanent feature, and today forms the backbone of the magazine. Third, the editors of *The Enigma* gradually became responsible for publishing the magazine on a monthly basis, maintaining extraordinarily high standards of puzzle construction, keeping up with voluminous correspondence and basically holding the organization together. In sixty-seven years there have been only six tireless editors, all of whom have given their services free of charge to the organization. The sixth and present editor began her tenure in November 1977. One editor, Rufus T. Strohm, alias Arty Ess, served for thirty years!

THE ENIGMA

The masthead from *The Enigma*, the official publication of The National Puzzlers' League. Members enjoy being "in the game."

The Enigma is a twelve-page magazine. News of the Krewe (the collective name of the membership) occupies one to two pages but the bulk of the publication is now the puzzles contained therein. Between 80 and 110 puzzles are published each month—all original constructions by Krewe members, and usually quite difficult. They represent varieties which are not generally found in any of the popular puzzle magazines nor in the puzzle columns of mass-merchandised magazines: anagrams, antigrams, beheadments, charades, cryptograms, curtailments, forms, heteronyms, linkades, literatims, palindromes, rebuses, reversals, spoonergrams, subers, transposals and others.

Here are examples of several of these varieties. A puzzle marked with an asterisk denotes one of particular difficulty—the answer is an obscure word, and should be attacked gingerly!

A few comments regarding the format of the puzzles and the rules governing them are necessary. The numbers in parentheses refer to the number of letters in the answer, or keyword. Clues pertaining to a specific keyword or part of a keyword are always capitalized: e.g., FOUR-FIVE: the four-letter word—the five-letter word; or ONE-TWO: first word or phrase—second word or phrase, etc. All words must appear in the second and third editions of the *Merriam-Webster New International Dictionary.*

BEHEADMENT: Removal of a keyword's first letter to form a shorter word.

(5, 4)

"Come right in," said the FOUR
As he opened the door.
"We're delighted you're staying the night:
The family FIVE
Is due to arrive—
Ghost-Host **He appears when the moonlight is bright."**

(6,5)

We all have surely ONE
There'd be a lot more fun
If there were much less TWO
Agreed-Greed **Among nations me and you.**

CHARADE: a keyword is broken down into two or more syllables.

(6)

Every ONE should act his TWO
Man-Age (Manage) **Which I ALL to do. Do you?**

142

(6)

Sexist primers limit Jane's
Horizons; she ONE cook and wash
And TWO and watch the baby while
Her man has all the fun, by gosh!
No wonder many Janes are ripe
For ALL, insulted by such tripe.

May-Hem (Mayhem)

CURTAILMENT: Removal of a keyword's last letter to form a shorter word.

(8, 7)

A creature I am of lethargic proclivity—
Friends tend to use the word "lazy" instead.
My practice when LONGER to any activity:
Just take a SHORTER and get into bed.

Aspiring-Aspirin

DELETION: Removal of any letter of a keyword, except the first or last, to form a shorter word.

(8, 7)

The manager's neat—he's compulsively dressy:
It irks him to see that his team is so messy.
Their locker room's cluttered—an EIGHT for their clothing,
Equipment and litter—it fills him with loathing.
What's more, they keep bumbling from inning to inning—
Score twenty to nothing, with visitors winning.
The fans (oh, those rude unappreciative creatures!)
Let loose with a SEVEN or two from the bleachers.

Catchall-Catcall

FIRST-LETTER CHANGE: First letter of keyword is replaced by another letter to form another keyword.

*(10)

"This stream is termed ONE," the geologist said,
"Erosional forces determined its bed."
But when waters rise and turn chocolate in hue,
The floods that result can be said to be TWO.

Indigenous-Undigenous

REBUS: A puzzle form in which letters, numbers and symbols represent words or phrases to which clues appear in an accompanying verse.

(5)

———JKLMEPQRS———

Stop that REBUS and quiet down;
People can hear you all over town.

Noise (NO is E)

143

(5, 8)

L S

200 colleges I've seen,
Of national parks at least 15;
And of the REBUS 44,
And hope I live to see 6 more.

Fifty Capitals (Fifty
Capital S)

(4 2 9 3 4)

L   C
L   U
U   R
P   B

Said the cop to the racer
"Just REBUS here.
Your speed's a disgrace, sir;
In court you'll appear."

Pull up alongside the
Curb

(3, 4)

ABDEFGHIJKLMNOPQRSTUVWXYZ

Call for a taxi, tell them, "Hey,
Have that TOTAL right away."

Cab Sent (C A bsent)

SPOONERGRAM: A puzzle involving the exchange of the initial sound of one word with that of another in a phrase.

(4 5; 4 5)

His pretty love was young, petite.
Her FIRST adorned by silken bow;
They shared sauterne, their joy complete;
Their kisses had a LAST, you know.

Tiny Waist-Winy Taste

TRANSPOSAL: The letters of one keyword are rearranged to form another keyword.

(9)

All those who claim they are not ONE
I must consider TWO
For each of us craves happiness,
Whatever else we do.

Hedonists-Dishonest

From its inception in 1883 until 1958 the National Puzzlers' League held biannual conventions usually in some Eastern city. Members residing in that city were responsible for hosting the convention. Activities consisted of puzzle competitions, speeches on puzzle construction or solving, banquets, sightseeing trips and opportunities to converse at great lengths with other puzzlers. From 1958 until 1976 there were no conventions because of lack of interest. However, in August 1976 a very successful convention was held in Princeton, New Jersey, followed

144

88th Semi-Annual Convention National Puzzlers League - Detroit, Michigan, Sept. 3-5, 1927

1. Myosotis. 2. Jack O'Lantern. 3. N. Jineer. 4. Lily May. 5. Bud. 6. Arty Ess. 7. Evero. 8. Mentor. 9. Hercules. 10. C. Saw. 11. Tyro. 12. Pearlie Glen. 13. See-wee. 14. Merlina. 15. Druh. 16. Gemini. 17. Ajax. 18. Primrose. 19. Phil Θ. Loger. 20. Gi Gantic. 21. Molemi. 22. Swamp Angel. 23. X. Specked. 24. E. Racer. 25. B. Natural. 26. Leip. 27. Merlin. 28. Merlo. 29. H. S. Nut. 30. Tante. 31. Eugene. 32. Calno. 33. Ronaele. 34. O. Min. 35. Jim Bill. 36. Nypho. 37. Ralph. 38. Sir Vare. 39. E. S. Crow. 40. Mazy Masker. 41. Cincinnatus. 42. T. Hinker. 43. Hi Kerr. 44. Artaxerxes. 45. Larry. 46. Spud. 47. Wick O'Cincy. 48. Chas. Essig. 49. Scan Daw.

one year later by an equally enthusiastic meeting in Buffalo, New York. It now appears that conventions will once again be an integral part of the NPL's activities.

What do puzzlers do en masse that make these conventions so much fun to attend? First, there are group names which involve everybody and are primarily oriented toward breaking the ice and getting conventioneers to meet each other. In the "Chain Game" that was played in Buffalo in 1977, each participant was handed an index card with the name of a famous lover on each side. The object was to find the two people who had the mates to your card and form a chain by linking hands. If your card read Cinderella and Agamemnon you were searching for Prince Charming and Clytemnestra. By the end of the game all members were entangled in one huge chain. Secondly, convention puzzle contests are arranged so that you can test your puzzle acumen against the other "pros" present. One such competition, "Fair and Square," necessitated composing fifteen six-letter word squares in twenty minutes. Here are the definitions for one of these squares:

1. Far-away light	Q U A S A R
2. Make current	U P D A T E
3. X-rated movie viewers	A D U L T S
4. Girl's name	S A L L I E
5. New York State prison	A T T I C A
6. Usher again	R E S E A T

Probably what puzzlers enjoy most at conventions is the chance to mingle for a weekend with people who are as passionate about puzzles as themselves. It's comforting to realize that one's addiction to puzzles and word games is not a malaise to be treated by the local psychiatrist but a highly respectable hobby shared by numerous other people.

Princeton Inn

Princeton, New Jersey

August 13 - 15, 1976

In each ring is hidden a familiar eight-letter word, running either clockwise or counterclockwise. Find the words, and draw a slash (/) between the first and last letters of each.

```
Ex.  E/P R    1.  I R O    2.  T O R
     S   I        C   T        A   E
     O R M        H I S        V E L

 3.  T I L    4.  A L S    5.  C H E
     R   I        N   I        O   T
     O T A        D E R        C I R

 6.  O B L    7.  I T S    8.  D N E
     N   E        C   Y        E   V
     N A M        A L M        R L A

 9.  P E R   10.  O R E   11.  I V O
     O   E        N   A        R   S
     A T T        A U T        T U O
```

ABOVE LEFT

The cover of the convention program for the 1976 NPL get-together in Princeton.

RIGHT

A serious sampling of solvers — 1976 NPL meeting.

Membership in a puzzle league such as the NPL enables one to associate with other puzzlers in many ways. Although the conventions were only recently reinstituted, members of the NPL have used the mails to become known to each other. Members are encouraged to write to each other about everything, puzzle-related or not, and many substantive friendships have been formed solely through the mail.

In the past, members of the NPL residing in the same city formed local puzzle clubs, which enabled members to challenge each other between conventions. Among the most famous and long-lived were the Diamond Club of Philadelphia, the Riddlers of New York and the Genessee Owls of Rochester. Although these original clubs have all disbanded, there have been recent attempts to revive the local club concept in the New York-New Jersey-Connecticut area.

NPL members range in age from 17 to 90. Their occupations run the gamut from engineer to musician, math consultant to housewife. Many are highly educated and tend to pursue solitary pleasures. Puzzling, by nature, is an activity one engages in alone. However, through membership in a league such as the NPL, puzzlers can expand their horizons by sharing their pastime with interested and interesting companions. The use of noms in signing puzzles and correspondence is an integral part of NPL etiquette. Although the use of real names is permitted, most members choose to address each other by their noms. These noms are unique and reflect the puzzler's hobby, occupation or lifestyle. NIGHTOWL is a person who functions best in the evening; SMITH, TIM S. is an expert on palindromes; TREESONG is a science fiction fanatic; and OSAPLE was born in El Paso. Using noms also serves to add to the mystique of the art of puzzling.

The American Cryptogram Association was formed in 1932 as an offshoot of the NPL. For years conventions were held jointly until in-fighting caused the two groups to become entirely separate organizations. Basically, ACA members derive the same benefits from their league as do NPL members: solving and constructing challenging cryptograms, corresponding with like-minded people and attending conventions and local puzzle clubs. Through *The Cryptogram*, the official magazine of the ACA, members are presented with cryptograms to solve from five major categories: aristocrats, patristocrats, cryptarithms, xenocrypts and ciphers. Ciphers are further broken down into approximately fifty types, including key phrase, ragbaby, tri-digital, checkerboard, homophonic, grandpre, bifid, slidefair, railfence and quagmire. Because the uninitiated would find it extremely difficult to decode the crypts and ciphers contained in the ACA magazine, only a few of the simplest cryptograms will be presented here.

ACA Cryptogram 1

UK UJ JIR KZ JLL ALZAOL JBNIYRLCUYS KTLUC XZYLF IYR WYZH FZN QIYZYK TLOA KTLX IOKTZNST FZN HZNOR QLCKIUYOF OUWL KZ

ACA Cryptogram 2

XR ITS VKCQ QCQL ATWXNQP, FVXDQ ETOW HQTHDQ FKAW WT MQ NKDDQP "ATLEKD," WVQI VKWQ WT MQ WVTSUVW TR KO "KCQLKUQ."

2. IT IS SAD TO SEE PEOPLE SQUANDERING THEIR MONEY AND KNOW YOU CANNOT HELP THEM ALTHOUGH YOU WOULD CERTAINLY LIKE TO.

1. IF YOU HAVE EVER NO-TICED, WHILE MOST PEOPLE WANT TO BE CALLED "NOR-MAL," THEY HATE TO BE THOUGHT OF AS "AVERAGE."

147

ACA members tend to be more letter-oriented than the word-oriented members of the NPL. Deciphering ability appears unrelated to education; one must be able to focus on the behavior of individual letters to break a code.

Many members are professional decoders and, in fact, were recruited for cryptanalytical work in World War II through their membership in the ACA. The United States Army Signal Corps, Military Intelligence Division, purposely subscribed to the ACA magazine prior to the United States' entry into the war to compile a list of the top solvers. These people were then contacted and asked if they wanted to receive formal training in cryptanalysis and enlist in the army. Sufficient members were patriotically inspired to use their skills for the government during this crucial period so that a decline was witnessed in the ACA rolls. Dave Shulman, the former contest and puzzle editor for King Features Syndicate who has been active in the ACA since its inception, was one of the members who took advantage of the army training to become a professional cryptanalyst. He spent the war years in the Aleutian Islands cracking Japanese codes.

Other members have distinguished themselves through their deciphering skills. BARBARA (a nom-de-plume) broke the Ché Guevara code which had stymied professionals for years. Many ACA members are engaged in occupations such as computer programming, mathematics and engineering that enable them to exercise their deciphering and coding skills.

Both the NPL and the ACA provide their members with immeasurable hours of sheer enjoyment, mental stimulation and friendship. For puzzlers who regard their pastime as a serious hobby and welcome the challenge of unusual puzzles, one or both of these leagues would be worth joining.

The British Scene:
A Leagueless but Lively Legacy

At present, America seems to have a premium on puzzle leagues, but organized puzzling is by no means an unheard of activity in the British Isles. By far the most active in the field of participatory puzzle promulgation is the firm of Cutty Sark Scotch Whisky. Their first foray into the arena of public puzzling was in 1970 when, in conjunction with *The Times*, they sponsored a National Crossword Championship based on *The Times* crossword. Eight years later the annual competition is still running strong, with thousands of entrants a year vying to get past the qualifying rounds into the regional finals and finally the national finals. The grand prize? A luxury holiday for two in Monte Carlo, a solid silver Cutty Sark Crossword Trophy and, last but not least, a half-gallon of whisky—Cutty Sark, of course!

Encouraged by the growing popularity of the crossword championships, Cutty Sark embarked upon a new puzzle project in 1977, this time in association with *The Guardian*. Remarkably similar both in form and feeling to the recently resurrected weekend-long annual convention of the National Puzzlers' League in America, the venture was billed as:

WORD WEEKEND

A mind-stretching marathon of word puzzles lasting two days and two nights.

INCORPORATING

THE CUTTY SARK / GUARDIAN

LOGOGRIPHIST OF THE YEAR

COMPETITION

A Positively Pleasurable Pot Pourri of Perplexing Puzzles Providing Provocation and Perturbation for the Post-Prandial Predilection of Participants. A Prodigious Package of Polysyllabic Posers and Philological Problems for your Perspicacious Perusal, to Promote Polemic and Permit the Presentation of a Plurality of Prizes!

In response, more than eighty word enthusiasts from all over Britain flocked to the Grand Hotel in Birmingham to take part in the country's "first ever festival of words." Featured in the program of non-stop entertainment were five 1½-hour sessions including enigmatic entertainments, word puzzles, pencil and paper puzzles, curious and quickie crosswords, harder-than-average crosswords, a spelling bee, a "Coin-a-Word" contest — apparently *logogriphist* wasn't good enough for the sponsors! — plus two Night Owl competitions for interested insomniacs (the puzzles were handed out at 11 P.M. and had to be submitted by 9 A.M. the following day). Presiding over the event as the weekend word arbiter was Dr. John Sykes, Deputy Chief Editor of the *Oxford English Dictionaries* and himself a five-time winner (and still going strong) of the National Crossword Championship. Emerging triumphant as "Logogriphist of the Year" was Mr. David Meadows of Alvaston, Derbyshire, who carted off the grand prize: the two-volume micrographically reproduced *Compact Edition of the Oxford English Dictionary* (with magnifying glass), a trophy and, of course, the ubiquitous half-gallon of Cutty Sark whisky. Winner of the "Coin-a-Word" competition was Mr. Norman Pritchard of Shelmersdale, Lancashire, for his entry "lancastration" — a rather painful operation undergone by Yorkshiremen, who suddenly found themselves part of Lancashire, thanks to local governmental reform. A toast is due to Cutty Sark for keeping puzzling alive and well in the British Isles, as it is elsewhere throughout the world!

PICTURE ANSWERS

COMING OF AGE

1 *Britannia to America*
My dear Daughter I cannot behold without great pain your headstrong backwardness to return to your Duty in not opposing all the good I long intended for your sole Happiness and being told that you have giv'n your hand to a base & two-faced French-man. I have sent you over five wise men the greatest of all my children to put you to rights and hope you will lis-ten to them and mind what they say to you they have instructions to give you those things you formerly required so be a good girl discharge your sol-diers and ships of war and do not re-bel against your mother rely upon me and do not trust to what that french Rascal shall tell you I see he wants to bring on an enmity to all unity be-tween you & I but listen not to him all the world takes notice of his two faces. I'll send him such Messages from my great cannons as shall make his heart repent and know that one good or ill turn merits another. NB let not hate take too much hold of your heart.
> I am your friend & mother

2 **Illustrated Rebus**
No. 4 Evil to him that evil thinks.
Enigmas
No. 3 Captain Mayne Reid
No.4 Toussaint l'Ouverture
Arithmetical Puzzles
No. 6 "half" of XLI (~~XLI~~) is VII + XXI = XXVIII   No. 7 NINE
Illustrated Rebus
No. 5 (Names of English Authors)

1 —Tennyson 2 —Ruskin
3 —Browning 4 —Carlyle 5 —
Jean Ingelow 6 —Dora Greenwell

3 The Engima is of such ancient and respectable origin, that I shall ask no one to excuse me for offering this tome to the public. Enigmatical ques-tions are frequent in the Scriptures, and in olden times often contained a great deal of valuable information.

4 **No. 444 – Conundrums**
When he is a rover.
Because it is the grub that makes the butter fly.
Because we must all give it up.
For divers reasons.
It is the fruit of good living.
A door bell.

No. 445 – Charades
a)gas-pipe; b)fire-light.

No. 446 – A Picture Puzzle
Black and white and red all over. A newspaper.

No. 447 – Numerical Enigma
H. Rider Haggard.

No. 448 – Articles of Furniture
a)bookcase; b)wardrobe;
c)washstand; d)sofa.

No. 449 – A Geographical Acrostic
a)Bengal; b)Ebro; c)Rubicon;
d)Lapland; e)Idaho;
f)Nankin. INITIALS = Berlin;
FINALS = London.

No. 450 – The Knight's Puzzle
Better to die with harness on
In smoke and heat of battle

Than wander and browse and fall
 anon
In quiet of meadow land cattle

Better to gain by arm or brain
Chaplet of laurel or myrtle,
Than bask in sun
With work undone
And live one's life
Like a turtle.

No. 451 – Proverbial "P"
Proscrastination is the thief of time.

No. 452 – Reversible words
a)reel-leer; b)dial-laid;
c)ten-net; d)tar-rat.

No. 453 – Quibbles
a)Draw it round his body; b)8¼;
c)Twice twenty-five is fifty; twice five,
and twenty, is thirty.

A PANOPLY OF PUZZLES PAST

5 a)Miguel de Cervantes Saavedra;
   b)Dante Gabriel Rosetti; c)Grover
   Cleveland; d)Little Red Riding Hood.

6 A tanner.

7 Because he makes notes.

8 Coriolanus, Othello, Hamlet.

9 Red Rum & Murder could be counted
   372 ways. Since the phrase is a palindrome, however, there are as many
   ways of counting it backwards. Thus
   the square of 372 gives a total of
   138,384 ways without any two ways
   being alike.

10 A bird in the hand is worth two in the
    bush. Be not weary in well doing.

11 When the bough breaks,
    The cradle will fall
    Down will come baby,
    Cradle and all.

12 To open gate push.

CROSSWORD CRAZE

13
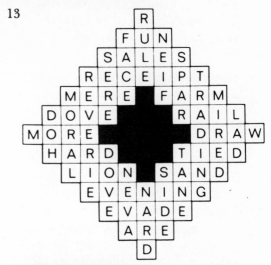

PUZZLE PROMO

14

Explanation of More Difficult Clues
Clues Across

1 WHISPERING not whimpering. Even
   though "stern," it does not mean the
   "father" is inconsiderate. Whimpering
   suggests distress of some sort, so he
   may well investigate first to be certain
   the children haven't suffered any
   harm, rather than just "reprimand"
   them. WHISPERING makes a clear-cut
   answer to the clue's context.

7 GLOSSY not glassy. "If" the "surface" of
   the "new table" is glassy, it has a vitre-
   ous finish which, "if scratched," *is*

"permanently" damaged. "If" the "surface" has a high polish (i.e. is GLOSSY) the "meticulous owner" can "hope it's not permanently" damaged by "scratching."

8 SHEDS not sleds. SHEDS is more apt for the clue word, "if," as they may or may not be "sturdily built" – they may be only temporary. Sleds have to stand up to jolting and generally rough treatment when running, so that they are, *of necessity*, "sturdily built" even to have a normal duration.

12 RICH not rice. "A RICH dish" is more to the point, with its strong appeal to the palate "of a heavy eater." But there is no indication in the clue whether he particularly likes rice: if he is not particularly partial to it, the "dish" would be *easy* "to resist."

16 BALD not bold. The clue is more apt of "a BALD denial," indicating there's nothing to back it up. The very conviction of "a bold denial" can indeed be convincing, which no doubt includes some supporting evidence.

17 LEAN not leap. "A leap year" is merely a calendar fact, not actually "describing" the *"year" itself*. "A LEAN year" is favored, as it points out how it differed from others. Lead is too vague.

19 DUNCE not dance. We are made so aware today through feature newspaper and magazine articles on learning disabilities, as well as in TV documentaries, that "the average novelist" would, surely, be exposed to the characteristics of "a DUNCE." The kind of dance needs to be qualified – there are so many in this country and throughout the world.

20 SILKY not silly. "The SILKY" (i.e. over-suave) sales "pitch," yes. But "in a true comic sketch," the "humor" would lie in the "victim's" *believing* "the pitch" that to anyone else is patently silly.

21 HATING not eating. HATING links di-

rectly with the clue phrase, "all the vile food." Furthermore, if it's *"vile,"* it's highly unlikely that the "soldiers" would be eating it "all."

Clues Down:

1 WAITER not writer. A WAITER, who is normally unaccustomed to the world of publicity and "TV," yes. However, a writer who must be well enough known to be "publicizing his memoirs," and "would probably" have already had considerable public exposure through promoting his writings. Why then should he feel "uncomfortable on TV" discussing "his" *own* "memoirs"?

3 PIKE not peke. A creature that has had to defend itself against enemies, if it survives, develops over the years a cunning which a domestic pet would never need, making PIKE more apt than peke.

5 GASHED not gassed. The horrific sight of blood flowing when the "soldiers" are GASHED is more likely to "make" a "deep impression on" a "sensitive child." If they're merely becoming unconscious from being gassed, the inward suffering is not something that the average "child" is aware of at his age.

6 JAY not bay. The gorgeous color of the JAY is the better answer, as it would be lost in "a black-and-white photo," making it look similar to many another bird. The build and strength of the bay horse could be impressively portrayed in black and white. Furthermore, the bay (horse) is usually dull-colored anyway.

9 GOOD not wood. It's the fact that it is "a GOOD," brightly blazing "fire" that makes the scene so enjoyable; what is burning (e.g. wood) is immaterial.

11 GIGGLING not goggling. If the "madman" is GIGGLING, he is either mentally reflecting on what he's done, or is about to do, which "may well" be

something "eerie," it being "a horror movie." Idly "goggling at the moon" doesn't "suggest" any *action* – he could be simply hypnotized by it.

13 CLEARLY not cleanly. "Having been CLEARLY beaten" (or thoroughly bested) is more apt for this positive clue and the "need to reestablish himself" as a top "boxer." Though "cleanly beaten," the decision could have been very close which would not seriously damage his reputation.

18 BEST not bent. "Sort out" suggests picking them out carefully to keep separately, favoring "the BEST nails." "Usually" he will *throw away* "the bent ones."

FAMOUS PUZZLE PEOPLE

15 *My dear Ina,*
Though I don't give birthday presents still I may write a birthday letter. I came to your door to wish you many happy returns of the day, but the cat met me, and took me for a mouse, and hunted me up and down till I could hardly stand. However somehow I got into the house, and there a mouse met me, and took me for a cat and pelted me . . .

16

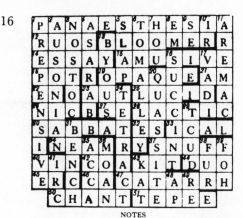

NOTES

Across: 12 rev. Sour(dine), mus.; 13. Mrs. Bloomer; 14. Ess-ay; 18. Ca-se; 28. No use crying over spilt milk; 30 & 33. Sabbatical-year Ba-al unchecked; 34. Mean; 40. Vin(age), addition of spirit to wine; 42. Co(efficient), alg.; 43. Inches, the size of Kneller's portraits for Kitcat Club; 44, Two's company, etc.; 50. Chant(age), blackmail.

Down: 2. Italian; 5. Scot., slap-up; 8 & 10. Mire; 11 rev. In camera; 16. Succin(C)t; 17. Vadi(um), Scots law, um(bo), the boss of a shield; 29 rev. Quoted by Harry Graham in *The Bolster Book*; 31. A judge; 36. Keith of Ravelston, Sydney Dobell; 39. Ham. II, 2, 625; 49. Ham III, 2, 4; 43. Ancient Egypt, cat; 49 & 48. Sour, âpre.

17 *From Alfred Lord Tennyson's "Ulysses"*

And tho'
We are not now that strength which in old days
Moved earth and heaven; that which we are, we are;
One equal temper of heroic hearts,
Made weak by time and fate, but strong in will
To strive, to seek, to find and not to yield.

A PANOPLY OF PUZZLES PRESENT

Puzzle 1

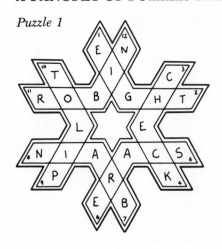

Puzzle 2

153

Puzzle 3

Puzzle 4

Puzzle 5

Puzzle 6

Puzzle 7

Puzzle 8

```
P R O V I D E O A R G L I B E F T
R E V E R E N D D E R I D E N O R
O V E R R A T E D L A M E D N E E
V A R Y E R R A T I C A S S U R E
E L L I P S E L A C E R A T I O N
D U E L A P P O R T I O N A P E D
D E A L R A R E P I N T D R A M A
E X P I A T E P A C T A N N U A L
S E R B B I N A R Y O B I A C R E
K N E E L A E R T E S A N T H E M
R O A R E L U S I V E R E T I R E
A P P A L P R O C E E D R I P E R
S H A L E I N N U E N D O L O P E
C O G U T T E R L E V I T Y L O W
A B O R T I V E A R I S E P A R A
L I N G E R E N R I C H W A T T S
S A Y E R E R O S E E Y E L A S H
```

Puzzle 9

Puzzle 10

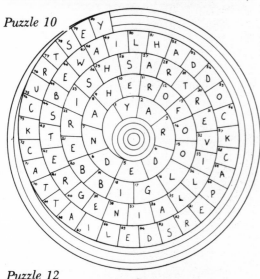

Puzzle 11

Puzzle 12

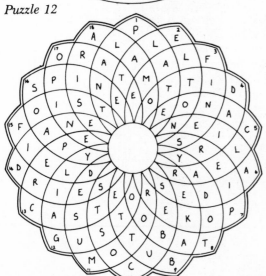

Puzzle 13

Puzzle 14

```
L E A F   A B U T   B R A S S
A X L E   S O R E   E A S E L
S T O W   L Y N X   S P I N E
S O U   S O   S A L T   A D D
O L D H A N D   S A M E
    A N G E R   P A Y O F F
D E F T   A B E T   N E V E R
I C E   S A P I D   E R E
S H E A R   R E N O   A N N E
H O L D U P   L E G A L
    E N O S   S T R E T C H
M A P   I T C H   I T   R O E
O C E A N   R E A R   G A L A
T R A I T   E R I E   O D O R
H E L L O   W O R D   T E N T
```

Puzzle 15

```
♡ T A W V T L H
B T J J D J H K
G J E E O O T U
P R H L D O N S
T J E S L A H D
R A L L N R J R
C W T A T A N T
R E U O A E A T
```

Puzzle 16

(3) FLAMINGO
(2) RUSTLER
(3) AUTOCRAT
(2) BANISH
(3) ELBERTA
(4) LAMENTATIONS
(2) ATTACH
(4) IRRADIATE
(3) STIPULATE
(2) STRATUS
(2) OBSTRUCT

(3) MEZZANINE
(2) URBANE
(5) CONDOMINIUM
(3) HERCULES
(2) IRISH
(4) SUKIYAKI
(4) ANTAGONISM
(4) METICULOUS
(3) AVARICE
(2) NEWSREEL
(3) WATERPROOF

Puzzle 17

1 Many a man is not superstitious because he thinks it brings bad luck.

2 If you look like your passport photograph you need the trip.

3 The man who thinks he knows everything always irritates those of us who do.

Puzzle 18

L	1 TABLES	2 BEAST	3 SATE	B
I	4 AIRING	5 GRAIN	6 RANG	I
N	7 RATED	8 TRADE	9 DATE	R
C	10 TRACED	11 RATED	12 DARE	T
O	13 HOARSE	14 SHARE	15 ERAS	H
L	16 MODELS	17 DOMES	18 SOME	D
N	19 PARENT	20 TAPER	21 PERT	A
S	22 SATYRS	23 TRAYS	24 STAR	Y

Puzzle 19

```
T A C K R O O M   T A K E O F F   P A D D O C K
H H U O V E R R G A I A I
O A T U A L S O R A N N M I L E R
R U M B L E N I H F T B
O P R E T A I N O P E R A B O A R D Y
U I H H O R R I N G
G O O D H A N D S I N F I E L D I A
H N N A P R O N I U V T
B S T U D S L N G E A S E
R H N N A R A G A N S E T T P A C E R T
E I L U N L H A A U
D I P P E D B A C K T A P A D E R O R M
A B F E R D U S T E
A D S I N N E R R E I N S O D A I R S
B R U S H N N Q E P S P A N P
O D C U S O D O N E A
U E T O P B E C H E R S B R O O K E A
T W O O A A S H X E X M O O R R
T H R O W S D L T O R S O
U A R A T T A I L R R A M E E T F
R N I C R R A L H O
N A G N I P T R A C E E N C L O S U R E O
L E G A O I N A T R U N
E I R D N S E O
R E C O R D S S T E M M O T H E R B A R
```

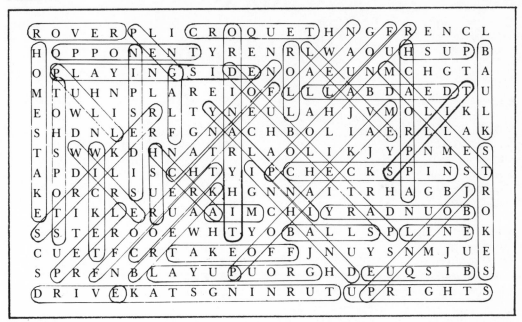

PICTURE CREDITS

Grateful acknowledgement is made to the following persons and companies for their permission to reprint illustrative material:

Aquarius Contests: 90

Cirencester Museum: 22

The Late C. L. Dodgson, Trustees of the Estate of,: 104

Mary Evans Picture Library: 20 (both), 25, 26, 27, 48, 50 (all), 53, 67 (both)

Fortune Magazine (July 1937): 88 (all)

Steve Gianakos: 138 (photographed at the Alessandra Gallery)

Hallmark Cards, Inc.: 139 (bottom)

Harcourt Brace Jovanovich, Inc.: 66 (bottom: from *Mother Goose Riddle Rhymes* by Joseph Low, copyright 1953)

Hodder & Stoughton Children's Books: 69 (from *First Knight Book of Puzzles* compiled by Falcon Travis)

Joe Hovanec: 146 (bottom)

Jesse Jacobs Associates: 96

King Features Syndicate: 125 (bottom: from *Encyclopedia of Puzzles and Pastimes*, ed. Clark Kinnard, copyright 1946)

Library of Congress: 12

Metropolitan Museum of Art: 11 (bequest of William H. Herriman, 1921), 18 (Expedition, 1930; detail)

National Library Publications: 91, 92, 93, 94

New Approaches, Inc.: 135 (both)

New York Public Library, Lincoln Center Collection: 76

New York Public Library Picture Collection: 21, 40

New York Public Library, Rare Book Division, Astor, Lennox and Tilden Foundations: 31 (all), 32, 55 (both), 56, 57 (top left), 66 (top and center)

The New York World: 73, 80

Penny Press: 113, 114, 115, 116, 117, 119 (bottom), 121, 122, 123 (both), 124, 125 (top), 126, 127 (both), 128, 129 (both)

Poynter Products: 139 (top)

The Puzzler: 118, 120

Saturday Review of Literature (March 31, 1934): 111

United Feature Syndicate, Inc.: 95

United Press International: 75 (right)

Max Walter Advertising: 97 (left)

Wide World Photos: 107

157

INDEX

159